When the ~~tough~~ breaks . . .

Hush-a-bye baby
  On the tree-top.
When the wind blows
  The cradle will rock;

When the bough breaks
  The cradle will fall:
Down will come baby,
  Cradle and all.

When the bough breaks . . .

*Giving your child security
in an insecure world*

Myra Chave-Jones

Inter-Varsity Press

INTER-VARSITY PRESS
38 De Montfort Street, Leicester LE1 7GP, England

Unless otherwise stated, Scripture quotations in this publication are from the Holy Bible, New International Version. Copyright © 1973, 1978, 1984 International Bible Society. Published in Great Britain by Hodder and Stoughton Ltd.

The poem on pp. 25–26 is from *Clearing Away the Rubbish* copyright © Adrian Plass 1988 with the permission of 'Minstrel', Kingsway Publications, Eastbourne, England.

The poem on pp. 55–56 is 'Disobedience', from *When We Were Very Young* by A. A. Milne, published by Methuen Children's Books and reproduced by permission.

First published 1994

British Library Cataloguing in Publication Data
A catalogue record for this book is available from the British Library.

ISBN 0–85110–877–6

Set in Palatino
Typeset in Great Britain by Parker Typesetting Service, Leicester
Printed in Great Britain by Cox & Wyman Ltd, Reading

Illustrated by Leigh Harrison

Inter-Varsity Press is the book-publishing division of the Universities and Colleges Christian Fellowship (formerly the Inter-Varsity Fellowship), a student movement linking Christian Unions in universities and colleges throughout the United Kingdom and the Republic of Ireland, and a member movement of the International Fellowship of Evangelical Students. For information about local and national activities write to UCCF, 38 De Montfort Street, Leicester LE1 7GP.

Contents

To my parents

in gratitude for the stable home
they tried to create for me

Acknowledgments

Glenys Barham, my niece, had been a constant help and encourager. Mary Sylvester's support and insightful criticisms have been immensely valuable. Jenny Hyatt has shared her time, her expertise and some of her personal experience in order to make the manuscript more readable. Philip and Anne Lovegrove have, from time to time, allowed me to hide out in their house so that I could write undisturbed.

I am grateful to my erstwhile teachers at the Tavistock Clinic in the Department for Children and Parents (now called the Child and Parents Department) and at the Family Discussion Bureau (now called the Institute of Marital Studies).

I would also like to thank the people who told me about their experiences both in childhood and as young adults, and the children who told me as much as they could articulate of their feelings and their life as they saw it. All these people have given me permission to quote them verbatim, although I have disguised the identities of some of them for obvious reasons.

Other people, too, have helped me in countless ways but are too numerous to mention by name.

Finally, I would like to thank my many friends who have borne with me so patiently while I was writing this book.

The way in

When I was asked to write about healing the wounds of a broken home and disrupted family, I thought I was on fairly familiar ground. Much of my professional life has been spent listening to and working with people who are in pain from their experience of life in childhood, with or without a family, and whose perception of themselves and reactions to the world are coloured by that pain. I know well about the anguish of such situations. So I began to address myself to the task of describing the importance of family life and the evil of broken homes.

But in no time at all I was in a morass, asking myself big questions. Many of these have originated in the twin revolutions of the twentieth century: the technological and the sexual. They have completely altered our way of life and our expectations and have made modern living unthinkable to our forebears. We now live in a world where many grandparents cannot understand the hobbies and the language of their grandchildren; where we can control the genetic processes to some extent; where the good of society gives way to the freedom of the individual; a 'brave new world' where words have lost their original meaning or have become relatively unknown.

The purpose of this book

Most books about divorce or a divided home are concerned with the adults. In this book we will concentrate mainly on the emotional effects upon the *children*. We hear a great deal from the media and the Government about the financial and social impact of family breakdown, but there is a significant absence of understanding of the *emotional* repercussions. This is the case in spite of the fact that so much knowledge is readily available to everyone.

A divided home is a hard place to struggle through. I have walked alongside many who have been through painful experiences and I have shared their feelings, and the anguish and struggles of the healing process. I have spoken to many children of various ages. Most of the young ones found it difficult to articulate how they felt, but they spoke in general terms about not liking the situation, feeling different from other children, not wanting to talk about it (because they don't know how to handle their feelings), but just wishing their parents would get back together again.

I was tempted to give up on more than one occasion as I sensed and shared some of the crippling fear and disconsolate loneliness that most of the children of divorced or separated parents suffered. Writing this book was painful for me personally.

There were two ways in which I could have avoided a head-on confrontation with this pain. One way would have been to give up – to withdraw from the situation, to stop writing. The other way would have been to deny the plight of the children, to say that they really do not suffer much and soon adapt to a new situation.

But the more I looked into the facts, the more I was sure that this is not the case. Children may not perpetrate outright rebellion, but they take their helpless confusion inside themselves, with distressing results. My sadness and anger *on behalf of the children* became a strong motivating reason for facing the pain, for continuing to write, at some personal cost. It is not possible to convey in print a child's tone of distress or look of utter confusion. Therefore, in my view, it is important to raise the level of awareness about the emotional processes and needs of a child in his or her early years, and about the vital contribution which *a stable home and marriage* make as the child grows up.

I want to try to help those adults who are struggling to keep their relationships and home together, to encourage those who are sliding about in dangerous places, and possibly to support people who are trying to help children who have been hurt.

If, at times, my readers think I am overstating the case, I ask them to bear with me. I can only say that through many years I have sat with countless people whose problems have originated from their relationship (or lack of it) with their parents. Perhaps it was a suffocating one or a loveless one or one in which they were not enabled to develop their own safe identity on a personal or sexual level. For this reason I care deeply about relationships within families. But I don't want to add to the sense of guilt which many parents feel when they are already doing their best. Since the world began there has never been a perfect parent.

'Unless you become like one of these . . .'

There is another compelling reason for spending time considering our children and the ways in which we influence them. Children are fascinating, aren't they? One minute so appealing and endearing, and the next an absolute nuisance! They are so wise, and their instincts are usually so accurate. Their honesty, sometimes embarrassing, is uncanny, and they seem to have an unerring 'sense of smell'.

It is no surprise that Jesus had a lot of time for children. I expect the winsome dynamism of his personality drew them to him, and he used them as a visual aid when he was trying to teach his grown-up, worldly-wise followers.

'You have to be like this', he said, referring to children's smallness, dependence and trustfulness, 'if you want to understand the kingdom of God and be part of it. If you are in control, independent and self-reliant, you will not be able to enter into the depths of the loving devotion and commitment that your Father in heaven shows towards you.

'But as you trust him, relate to him and get to know him, you will be able to develop an appropriate independence in accordance with your relationship with him. You will no longer need to behave child*ish*ly when you have become an adult. But until you are able to be dependent and child*like*, there is no possibility of your ever becoming a fully mature and spiritually aware adult.'

A map of our journey

This book is in no sense a manual on child care; neither is it a theological exposition. It is an attempt to bring before people's attention some of the important issues involved in the emotions of a growing child, and, I hope, to stimulate thought and careful consideration.

During our journey together we shall look closely at the nature of the bond between a child and his or her parents, in infancy, childhood and adolescence. This will lead us naturally into examining the immediate or long-term impact of the broken relationship on the child. We must, inevitably, take a look at marriage and some of the factors which precipitate breakdown. As we consider these things in the light of our Christian faith, we may have some hard and painful issues to face.

On the one hand, we may not want to accept some of the implications that are raised about the care of our children, because they may be personally inconvenient or the price which they ask of us may be too high. It would be easy under those circumstances to dismiss such implications with responses such as, 'Children are very resilient' or 'That's old-fashioned.' But we do at least have to know clearly what is involved, to make choices about our actions and to take personal responsibility for them.

On the other hand, we may feel encouraged and heartened to press on through difficult patches of the journey, drawing on unexpected spiritual and emotional resources.

Healing?

I was asked, initially, to write primarily about healing the wounds inflicted on children by the splitting up of their parents. This I declined to do. In my view, it is more sensible to talk about the possibilities of prevention rather than healing. In order to do this we have to look at *the nature and causes of the pain*. But, of course, we must also look at the subject of healing and what that involves.

Sometimes, Christians seem to find it very hard to tolerate the idea of physical or emotional pain, or else they seem to want to reduce it to a purely spiritual phenomenon. There seems to be a great desire to rush for short cuts to healing and growth. There are no short cuts in this case, but God does sometimes enable some of the stages to be smoothed.

I am glad to say that some of the children with whom I have talked are now showing signs of having made a tremendous improvement. Most of them have been surrounded by much prayer and careful love, and the wounds do seem to be healing. Nevertheless, they have to live with a fact in their life-story which will never change and which has left indelible marks.

We live in a less than perfect world. We all have emotional wounds, and so healing is very important to us. When there is disruption of the family, whether it is by unhappy relationships, separation, divorce or death, the wounds obviously vary in intensity according to the conditions. But there is never a situation in any family where there are no wounds at all. Some people seem to heal well and others take a lifetime, but there are often scars which are deeply hidden. Healing is about how we live with the scars so that they do not cripple and spoil the whole of the rest of our lives.

So, as we travel along our path together, through the ups and downs, our objective is to deepen our understanding of the suffering of children in family breakdown and to strengthen our commitment to love our God with all our heart, soul, strength and mind and to love our neighbour (*i.e.* our spouse or our child) as ourselves.

Note

In the interests of readability I have generally used the pronounce 'he' and 'him' when referring to an unnamed child. It should be understood that such references apply to boys and girls equally, and that no bias is intended.

Families under scrutiny

In a television programme entitled *Not the Nuclear Family*, broadcast in December 1991, four generations of one family appeared. Emily was 73, Joyce was 54, Annette was 27 and Anna-Marie was 10.

Emily was brought up in a traditional Victorian home, the eldest of four living children. She married at the age of twenty and had ten children herself. Her life was confined to the house and the family, and she had no freedom. She did all the family washing by hand in an old bath-tub. Asked about her attitude to her husband, she said, 'He ruled the house. What he said went.'

Joyce, born in 1937, was married at eighteen and had five children. She lived in the same house all her married life and thought it a great improvement on her mother's. She had running water and a washing-machine. Joyce was given away at her wedding by her father. In fact, if her father had not approved there would have been no wedding at all. 'If he shouted you moved,' said Joyce, 'and he only shouted once.'

Annette was born in 1964. Her main interest in life was listening to loud rock music. At seventeen, already pregnant, she married a guardsman, and was divorced a few years later. Joyce was 'devastated' about it; it was 'the end of part of our family life'.

Anna-Marie was born in 1981, and Joyce was (justifiably) afraid that Annette would not be able to look after her properly. Annette had found that she could not stay at home all day: there was 'nothing to do' and she was desperate to get back to her friends at work. So Anna-Marie was in the care of a daily child-minder. Asked by the interviewer if she minded her mother not being there when she came home from school, Anna-Marie said quite calmly, 'I always go to the child-minder, and Mummy collects me when she come home from work.'

'Do you mind not having your Daddy at home?'

'No,' replied conforming Anna-Marie, 'just partly.'

'Are there other children in your school who don't live with their daddies?'

'Yes, a few of them are divorced, but most of them live with both their parents.'

'Your Daddy's married again now and you've got a little sister,' said the interviewer brightly. 'How do you feel about that?'

There followed a fairly long pause. Then she said, 'Strange. But I've got used to it now.'

'Are you jealous?'

At this Annette at once replied for Anna-Marie: 'No. You like her and she's kind to you, isn't she?'[1]

This television programme illustrates how the expectations and experiences of family life have undergone a complete shake-up in the space of four generations.

Family life? Is there such a thing? What is it, anyway?

When so many people are complaining about the destructive influence of one or both of their parents or their hatred of a brother or sister, who needs family life?

Ought we to have a Government Department to help create and support better families? How would they go about it? Would it make any difference?

Divorce is so commonplace now: shouldn't we

apply our minds to making it easier and less traumatic, rather than trying to prevent it?

As these questions show, the way into the broken-homes scenario is complex.

The parent–child bond

We hear a great deal about the devastation that broken homes create, but some homes are, in fact, quite unfit for children to live in. Why is it that children cling to their parents so urgently, even when they are ill-treated, underfed and often abused in ways which make the rest of us feel shocked and angry?

The other day I had to go into a downtown supermarket for a pint of milk. (Of course, I came out with a dozen other things as well!) On my journey up and down the aisles looking for the milk, I saw a young woman with fair, tousled hair and dishevelled clothes, pushing an infant in a buggy. The baby dropped his dummy, so, after treading on it, the young woman (presumably, but not definitely, the child's mother, because her skin was a different colour from his and she was wearing a profusion of rings on her fingers) picked it up, licked it and shoved it back into the baby's mouth. A small girl, equally dishevelled, trailed along behind whimpering miserably. Suddenly the young woman flashed out an arm and cuffed the girl's head, swearing and shouting at her to be quiet, in colourful language which the girl obviously understood. There was silence for a few moments while the young woman marched angrily on. The little girl stood rebuffed, holding her burning ear and looking even more miserable. Then she continued her now silent and unpromising trail behind the other two.

What made her go on following? Why did she not just run off or shuffle away and wait at the shop door if she could not get home on her own?

What goes on between a parent and a child which creates such a strong bond? The strength of the bond is even more surprising when it is continuously negative and the child seems to receive little affection. Some women have experienced such bad mothering themselves that they have no idea how to be a mother to someone else; yet their children cling to them. Why do children who live with inadequate or even unkind parents still prefer to live with them rather than with anyone else?

Are parents interchangeable?

I wondered where that young woman's husband was, if she had one. Perhaps he was at the pub swilling beer with his mates, or at home watching the telly, or hard at work somewhere. I wondered how he would like to be landed with two fractious children all day every day.

But not all fathers are inadequate. One can often see fathers out shopping with their children, and all seems well and happy. It is a joy to see fathers cradling their tiny babies and caring so gently for them. It is not unheard of to encounter a 'house-husband' who stays at home to look after the house and family while his wife goes out to work.

So are parents interchangeable now? What does 'mothering' mean, if a father can do it just as well? Is there something special about being a mother, or about being a father? Can an au pair fulfil the same functions if necessary?

The Christian family

What is the difference between an ordinary family and a Christian family? Indeed, is a Christian family not ordinary? There is a little family living fairly near to me who look ideal. They have their ups and downs, of course, but the parents seem to be loving and very sensitive in the way they handle their children. I often hear great peals of laughter as they play together, and I sometimes see Dad taking the children out in the car while Mum presumably does something for herself. They are not extravagant in their lifestyle, and they take a great interest in green issues and the plight of the underprivileged. They never go to church, nor do they seem to know much about the Bible, but they are honest, caring and generally good-living people. How are they different from a Christian family, and what may be expected of a Christian family which may not be expected of a non-Christian family?

Something other than divorce

Broken homes are caused not only by divorce. There is, of course, the old enemy death, which wreaks its own particularly tragic form of havoc.

More common is the phenomenon of the single-parent family where there has never been a functioning father and the concept of a family with two parents is beyond the child's comprehension. We see many lone parents struggling to make ends meet and to carry the impossible burden of being both mother and father to the children.

Sister Margaret Walsh is a Roman Catholic nun who works in Wolverhampton. From her flat one can see most of the estate where she works: nine tower blocks, each twenty-two storeys high. Over 80% of the population, which is largely composed of teenage single parents, is on Social Security benefits. Most of the tenants are behind with their rent.

Sometimes both parents are present, but the atmosphere is such that the children live in a permanent state of anxiety. They hear constant rows and acrimony and they never really feel emotionally safe. The family is not physically broken, but the family atmosphere is torn into shreds.

Have God's purposes changed?

Society seems to be in a state of confusion these days. Marriage is no longer a binding commitment; divorce and infidelity are commonplace; young children are introduced to adult sexual behaviour by means of abuse; people do 'strange' things with their sexual orientation; young children commit appalling atrocities; justice seems to have gone haywire; when filling in an official form we are asked to state the name of our 'partner', who may be our husband or wife, or someone with whom we are living just at the moment, or someone we intend to live with for a long time but not to marry, or it may be someone of the same sex with whom we are living in a close and permanent relationship. Standards which were once clear-cut now seem to have acquired a permanent shade of grey.

Attitudes such as these are common today:

'If I get married to someone but a decent degree of relationship and compatibility fails to become established, does "Thou shalt not commit adultery" still apply? Can I be expected to stay in a loveless marriage when a more attractive relationship with someone else becomes a possibility?'

'I have seen what a mess my parents have made of their marriage, and I don't want the same to happen to me, so I shall just live with my partner. If it works out, we may marry later on. Besides, it's financially advantageous to stay unmarried.'

'I have a very good job: it's well paid, interesting and challenging. I worked very hard to get qualified and have a career. I am married and certainly want to have a family in due course. Then I'll stay at home to look after the baby for the first few weeks, but after that I shall pay a child-minder to look after it.'

'I am not really attracted in a sexual sense to members of the opposite sex, but I have a very loving relationship with my same-sex partner. Surely this is better than living alone in misery? We might even try to adopt a child at some stage. We could offer a child an excellent home.'

What are we to make of all this?

2

To have and to hold

One evening when I was busy in the local laundrette, I could not help overhearing the conversation between the assistant on duty and one of the other regulars.

'So you're actually getting married, then?'

'Yeah,' he replied drearily, rolling his chewing-gum around his mouth. 'Give it three years. That'll be about it.'

I could not resist a surreptitious glance at this engaging groom, and was tempted to think he was being over-optimistic! Normally, however, people go into their marriage with rather higher hopes than that.

Mark and Lucy certainly did.

An ideal marriage

It was a brilliant Saturday afternoon in mid-June. The church was reverberating to the strains of Widor's *Toccata*. Mark and Lucy walked down the aisle with their retinue, smiling and nodding at all the guests and revelling in the fact that this long-planned and all-consuming event was now safely accomplished. A few more hours of photographs, reception, speeches, kisses and congratulations, and then they could be off to their secret destination, to be together without intrusion from the outside world and its concerns.

They had thought seriously about their wedding vows 'made in the name of God who is judge of all and who knows all the secrets of our hearts'. They had not had much difficulty in saying, '. . . to have and to hold

from this day forward; for better, for worse, for richer, for poorer, in sickness and in health, to love and to cherish, till death us do part, according to God's holy law; and this is my solemn vow'. This is just what they intended to do with such delight. They had had some arguments, but they could not bear to be at logger-heads with one another, so they had struggled to work out their problems. They were desperate to belong to one another and spend their lives together, so the thought of being unfaithful seemed highly unlikely and remote: these colossal promises seemed a welcome commitment.

They had bought a little house and were having fun and a fair amount of frustration doing it up. They were planning to make their marriage an equal partnership, both taking shares in the domestic chores and financial responsibilities. They had a picture of their lives together for a year or two, or perhaps three, and then their little family of one, two or maybe three children. Then they might move into something bigger.

Mark and Lucy were both Christians and were heavily involved in the youth work of the local community in whose church they had just been married. They seemed to have everything going for them and the onlookers thought of them as 'a super Christian couple' – young, healthy, intelligent, committed and radiant. The hymns, prayers and address at their wedding had been full of praise and dedication to God and to each other in the future, as they rejoiced in God's will in bringing them together.

How thing turned out

And so it was. The first year or two went by. Mark was under great pressure in his job and worked long hours. The spectre of redundancy was always in the air, even for the most unexpected people. He left home early in the morning and usually returned twelve hours later, exhausted and drained. He often fell asleep watching the television. But his firm was very demanding of its staff in its attempt to keep solvent, and the mortgage had to be paid, so he had little choice.

Lucy also worked hard, often with unsocial hours, as a reporter for a local newspaper. It was a job that she enjoyed immensely and did well. She was on call quite a lot and had to work to deadlines most of the time. She was usually tired and often came home late in the evening.

They never seemed to get a chance to talk to one another these days. Lucy had not expected that it would be quite like this. But at least they had the weekends together in which to do the shopping and occasionally have a special meal or go to the theatre. That was fun. Sundays often felt as much like hard work as the other days of the week because of their church commitments, but at least they were involved in them together.

Their sex life, which had been so passionate and delirious at first, gradually lost a bit of its excitement in the general tiredness and stress of life. Lucy began to find it a bit boring and routine, but she did not want to hurt Mark's feelings, so she said nothing. On several levels they began to take one another for granted.

Then Lucy became pregnant. They were both delighted. Lucy worked for seven months and planned to take her full maternity leave. Thomas was born, and after initial feeding struggles they settled down together to a routine. But Thomas seemed not to need much sleep, and often cried in the night. This posed a dilemma. Mark needed his sleep, so he tended to leave the 'night shift' to Lucy because 'you're at home all day'. Lucy began to resent this, because being at home all day was no sinecure, and, what was more, she was missing her colleagues and all the stimulation of her job. Once she was awake, she could not get back to sleep again, whereas Mark was flat out as soon as his head touched the pillow.

Lucy was a new mother, inexperienced and not very sure of what to do. All the conflicting advice of well-intentioned friends confused her, and Mark was not available most of the time to share her anxiety. No-one had warned her how tiring it was to feed and care for a baby and how there was not much time for anything else, or how toddler-care can sometimes be exasperating and boring. But it was lovely to have this beautiful baby, on whom they both doted, to wheel out in his buggy, and there were times of great bliss when she was feeding him.

Eventually she decided not to go back to work, because she could not combine the job with the quality of care that she wanted to give to Thomas. In the course of time, Hugh, and later Clare, were born. Lucy found that she was completely taken over by motherhood. She felt as though she was at everyone's beck and call, and at times she was increasingly resentful that Mark seemed to be wedded to his job, thus leaving the brunt of the parenting to her. But she had to admit that at the weekends, Mark was certainly a good father to the children.

Mark argued that he had to work hard because of the pressure to supply the family with what they expected: a mountain bike for Thomas, a computer for Hugh, violin lessons for Clare, holidays for them all. And when the family had all these things there was a seemingly endless demand for more. All the other children at school had them, so Mark had to see to it that his children were not left out.

The Sunday routine still went on, though there were sometimes loud protests from the children that it was all a bit confusing. No doubt they would have echoed the sentiments of Adrian Plass's poem 'The Real Problem':

Sunday is a funny day
It starts with lots of noise.
Mummy rushes round with socks,
And Daddy shouts, 'You boys!'

Then Mummy says, 'Now don't blame them,
You know you're just as bad.
You've only just got out of bed,
It really makes me mad.'

My Mummy is a Christian,
My Daddy is as well.
My Mummy says 'Oh, heavens!'
My Daddy says 'Oh, hell!'

And when we get to church at last,
It's really very strange,
'Cos Mum and Dad stop arguing
And suddenly they change.

At church my Mum and Dad are friends,
They get on very well.
But no-one knows they've had a row,
And I'm not gonna tell.

People often come to them
Because they're very nice,
And Mum and Dad are very pleased
To give them some advice.

They tell them Christian freedom
Is worth an awful lot.
But I don't know what freedom means
If freedom's what they've got.

Daddy loves the meetings,
He's always at them all.
He's learning how to understand
The letters of St Paul.

But Mummy says, 'I'm stuck at home
To lead my Christian life.
It's just as well for blinking Paul
He did not have a wife.'

I once heard my Mummy say
She'd walk out of his life:
I once heard Daddy say to her
He's picked a rotten wife.

They really love each other.
I really think they do.
I think the people in the church
Would help them – if they knew.'

The end of the story?

Fifteen years passed. Lucy was now seeing a solicitor
about suing for divorce. The frustrations and neglect,

the loneliness and the anger of years, had all become too much for her. Unlike the majority of divorced wives, she was relatively independent financially, and was quite prepared to work to help maintain herself if necessary. She decided that she had a right to a life of her own. She was coming up to forty and was not prepared to spend the rest of her life tied to a man who, she thought, regarded her as a secondary consideration. It had all seemed so promising at first, but obviously she had made a mistake, she told herself. They did not seem to have anything in common any more.

She had wept and agonized over this decision. It was a drastic thing to do and was such a disappointing outcome to a glowing start. She had expected more of Mark and of marriage. Where had she gone wrong? She had forgiven five hundred times and more, but it was becoming hard to go on accepting Mark's demands for consideration and comfort when he seemed to pay no attention to *her* needs. He seemed to have time for other people's, though, and that irritated her.

She could not bear to think of the effect divorce might have on the children. She herself had come from an unhappy home, so she had first-hand experience.

Mark thought she was being unreasonable. There really wasn't a problem. Hadn't he done his best to provide for the family? What more could he have done? After all, he was the *only* breadwinner! Was this to be his reward? Every married couple has disagreements. Why did Lucy have to make such a big deal of it? Why could she not show a bit more understanding about his obligations and ambitions, of which she was a part? When Lucy complained that she could never talk to him, he responded by saying that if they did ever try to talk abut their relationship, the conversation would end up in violent recriminations and she would storm off, usually in tears; so there was not

27

much point in trying to talk. She was being impossible!

Lucy said her love was dead, and 'A marriage is over when the love has gone out of it.' But Mark was devastated. He was aware that the emotional atmosphere had changed, but he was not prepared for a unilateral declaration of independence. He tried persuasion, reason, promises, reform, even counselling, and everything he knew, but it was too late from Lucy's point of view. He did not believe that divorce was the answer to a marriage breakdown, from a Christian standpoint. It was true that his Christian 'commitment' had been largely superficial for some time; he had been going through the motions automatically rather than responding from his heart. He had been so busy and so tired and preoccupied. But now, he wanted to struggle with his problem from a Christian position. Lucy had heard all his propositions before, however, and she was reluctant but adamant this time. It had all been a mistake, and it was pointless and un-Christian to go on in an atmosphere of mutual destruction, she said. And so they separated and later divorced.

This situation had been creeping up on them for years, as they had, by default, ceased any constructive communication with each other. Neither really knew the inner needs and longings of the other any more. Lucy did not know how to cope with Mark's seemingly obsessional need to be popular and a success; Mark overlooked Lucy's deep inner need for mothering and affirmation. Those colossal vows they had made with such enthusiasm were finally declared officially null and void. God's will seemed to have veered off course.

So that was the end. But the trouble with divorce is that it does not really solve anything. It just creates a new set of problems which have a nasty habit of living on.

3

From dream to nightmare

In the months and years before Mark and Lucy finally split up, Thomas, Hugh and Clare were caught in the crossfire. They felt like flotsam and jetsam, not really knowing what was happening to them.

Clare had vivid memories of lying in bed listening to the angry shouting of her parents downstairs. Sometimes she had put her head under the pillow in an attempt to shut it out. When it went on for too long, she had shouted in desperation, 'Oh, *shut up*, you two!' This was a memory she wished she could forget. Once, Daddy had come in and said, 'Sorry, darling. We didn't mean to keep you awake.'

He was followed by an angry Mummy, who declared, 'It's all Daddy's fault.'

It had all been so painful, and had frightened her. She had so much wanted to make things better between her parents, but somehow it had not worked.

Thomas had been told about the impending divorce by his mother as gently as she could break such devastating news. He had known about the 'vicious and violent rows', and sometimes the stony silences, of course. He used to go out of the house and stay away for hours so that he would not hear it all. He had felt helpless and miserable. He had tried to understand what was happening, but he could not fathom the reasons for this drastic action of divorce. He was utterly confused. He hated the whole idea and felt very hurt and angry. He could not tell anyone about his inner pain, but just kept it inside himself. He knew that many other children go through the same experience, but you always hope it won't happen to you, and he felt ashamed about it.

Hugh, also, had been told by his mother about the divorce. He had been very frightened by the arguments and shouting and the times when things had been thrown around. He had just crept up to his room in misery, wondering what was happening. Hugh thought that somehow this was all his fault. He remembered the times when his mother had shouted at *him* because he had done something or other which displeased her. In his confusion and unhappiness, and from the self-imposed banishment of his room, he had felt sure that this disturbance was all due to something he had done, but he could not work out what it could have been. He had spent long hours searching the corners of his memory and his thoughts, but could not resolve this horrible problem. He had cried a great deal, and when, at times, he had seen both his parents crying, he had found it unbearable and very frightening. It felt as though his world had come to an end. Eventually, he found another boy at school whose parents had divorced three years previously, and together these two young lads tried to console one another.

Torn between the two

Five or six years later, with the children in their teens, Mark and Lucy's paths had gone in different directions. They both married again, and Lucy had another child, Vicky. But the catastrophe rumbled on. The custody of the children had been given to Lucy, who, with her new husband Michael, provided a good and secure base for them. To all intents and purposes it seemed that Thomas, Hugh and Clare had accepted the situation and adjusted reasonably well. Mark had struggled determinedly to keep in regular fatherly contract with them, but 'struggle' was the right word. Lucy's new way of life made it difficult to co-operate in shared custody times, and there was often a feeling of outrage for both Mark and Lucy individually. Frequently, Mark thought that it would be easier just to opt out and simply to send them messages and presents. But he loved his children and genuinely wanted to keep in touch with them in a good relationship, especially during their growing years.

On one occasion, Clare was asked by her father to decide where she wanted to spend part of her school holidays. There were fun and friends with her Mum and a different kind of fun and friends with her Dad. Which did she want? She had to decide today because the tickets had to be bought if she wanted to go with Dad. Clare was reduced to a paralysed heap of indecision, and eventually burst out in passionate sobs, 'How can I decide? I want to be with you both. No-one should ever be put in the position of having to choose which parent to be with. They should both be together.' And all the hidden pain surfaced again.

Hugh felt different from the other boys at school. He thought they did not understand his fragmentation, and was embarrassed when he had to explain to them that he was 'going to see Dad today'. He felt he had to try to please both parents; he had to guess how each would respond to any given situation, and pitch his own response accordingly. 'They both see things differently and they don't get together to sort things out. I don't know why they got divorced. They both give a different story and I don't know who to believe. I live in a permanent state of confusion. I feel powerless and torn between them both because I love them both. I can't make any sense of it. I don't understand and I don't like it, but that's how it is.'

When Mark had first moved out of the house, Hugh could not settle down at school. On occasions he just walked out of lessons because he could not concentrate or sit still any longer. The teachers knew the domestic situation and allowed Hugh to make his grieving protest. His school work deteriorated noticeably. He found it hard to work because of 'this big hole', though eventually he did make a half-hearted effort to catch up. He still functioned well below his potential, however, and had generally poor school reports.

Hugh now had three homes: one belonging to each parent, and the boarding-school to which he had been sent after the divorce. 'I don't belong anywhere. I can never give my friends a specific phone number because I can never be sure where I shall be. I find it very difficult to have to keep adjusting to different settings and what is expected in each place. It's all so confusing. I just try to adapt to whatever circumstances I find myself in and conform. I was very angry at first, but it's no good; so I just have to accept it. Michael doesn't do anything against me. He is kind and helpful, but I think he is "wet". I try to be nice to him because I can't do anything about it. But he's not like Dad. I love both my parents. It's sad to see the way Dad is changing in the new set-up. But he can't do anything about it, so he just has to accept it. I don't understand why Jesus had to make all this happen to us. I did find it hard but I don't think about it now. I just get on with life. But I am very frightened if my parents and their new partners ever start arguing.'

Searching for security

Thomas had been very quiet but unsettled for a long time after the divorce. A year or two later he was in big trouble because of his persistent stealing from people at school. There was no material reason why he should do this except that his pent-up anger and confusion had to explode somehow, causing maximum anxiety and distress to all concerned, and his parents in particular. Soon after the trauma of this episode, Thomas 'got converted'. He was longing for something that was 'stable, unchangeable and certain' and he seemed to sense that he would find it in the love of God. He said that he was 'wandering about in a fog before that; I couldn't see what life was about and didn't know what to do'. But now he felt much more 'confident inside'. He still felt numb about his parent's situation, but tried not to think about it. He 'kept his head down and his mouth shut'. In conversation with his parents, he was very wary so that he did not upset either party. He never gave anything away about his feelings and reactions or even about what he saw or heard in one house when he visited the other.

He really hated going to the two new weddings. It all seemed so strange and it made his parents' divorce so final. Right up till then, he had hoped that somehow or other there might be some reconciliation and that they would get together again. He was also very distressed and angry for a long time when his mother became pregnant in the new marriage. He grew to like little Vicky, however, but said he could never love her as a sister.

What does he think of marriage for himself, eventually? 'Oh, no. I don't believe in marriage any more.' So what does he think he might do? He doesn't know, but he is quite sure that he would not want to put anyone else through the misery that he had been through. He might live with someone on a casual basis, but he certainly would not want children.

Mark and Lucy both knew what damage can be done to the emotions and attitudes of children by the breakup of their home life. The children knew well that they were loved very much by both parents. Mark and Lucy had both assured each of them that there was no emotional problem that they could not discuss; but, on that score, the parents had no idea how far from the facts they were! It was probably never stated overtly, but at times two of the children seemed to be quite demanding of their parents' financial resources, almost as though they were wanting some sort of compensation. There were times when the parents felt guilty, too, and were over-indulgent. Also, they were aware of the danger of using the children as weapons against each other, but, in moments of exasperation over access difficulties, it was hard not to express their feelings in this way.

What hope?

All three children are now growing into adulthood with this spectre hanging over their heads all the time. There is no likelihood that the external circumstances will change. To the casual observer, these young people seem well adjusted, socially mature, intelligent and happy. But under the surface they carry their hidden sorrow and anger which they cannot express fully to the people concerned. So they bury it within themselves in its raw state: their sense of confusion; their acquired habit of keeping their feelings to themselves because it is not safe to be open about them; their sense of underlying emotional insecurity; their negative attitude to marriage and commitment; together with a very unsatisfactory basis from which to struggle with their own problems and disagreements in relationships. All this is not obvious at first glance, but it is there; and feelings do not go away if they are not dealt with. They may explode with various degrees of ferocity on future occasions. Thomas, Hugh and Clare will be able to rectify some of these difficulties if they make satisfactory friendships as time goes by, but they seem to be starting off with in-built disadvantages.

Variations on the general theme of Mark and Lucy's story are all too familiar: high hopes, and indeed many prayers, ending in distress and confusion. We are left with questions. Divorce: is it more acceptable now that most of us are no longer released from our marriage vows by the early death of a spouse? Marriage: how can we guarantee the success that most of us would want? Families: what sort are we looking for, and are they all that important? Children: is a broken home really such a time bomb or are we just making a fuss over something that isn't really that bad? And 'Why does Jesus have to make all this happen to us?'

We shall look at some of these questions in subsequent chapters.

4

The foundations

Let's start looking at the setting in which the time bomb of a broken home is placed.

What is a child? An adult in miniature? The physical stature would suggest this, but we need to look far more closely inside this question, to which the answer seems both obvious and yet obscure. It is very difficult to define precisely what a mother or a child is without concentrating mainly on their roles. But let us try to see what little boys and little girls are made of (apart from slugs, snails, puppy dogs' tails, or sugar and spice and all things nice, as the old stereotyping rhyme goes).

The baby's feelings

Painful feelings

There can be no doubt that the feelings of a child, however tiny, are very strong indeed. Sometimes there is great passion when the baby is screaming at full pitch, screwing up fists and kicking legs with all the intensity the little body can muster. All this can be very frightening for the baby, who feels as though he or she is tearing the world to pieces. Then again, even a small child experiences feelings of intense grief and sadness. The degree of inconsolable distress over the loss of a favourite toy may seem out of all proportion to a big grown-up who has had many experiences of anxiety over losing things and then the relief of finding them again. But the child has not lived long enough to have accumulated all this wisdom, and cannot easily be comforted by glib reassurances. There is also inevitable and real grief and anxiety over the temporary loss of mother when she is not available on demand, and the child feels lonely and even frightened or desolate without her.

Exciting feelings

In addition to feelings of fury or grief there are also, sometimes, observable feelings of intense eroticism which every baby experiences. These are particularly strong during excretory experiences and during breast-feeding. There is the anticipatory excitement, the experience of guzzling during the feed or internal activity during the excretion, the feeling of gratification afterwards and the relaxation of tension in satisfaction, with the glowing sublimity of inner contentment as the baby falls asleep. The accepting mother is also involved in the excitement (unless she is afraid of it or disgusted by it for some reason) and shares it with her baby, thus making the feelings additionally enjoyable. (This sequence of feelings will be aroused at a much later stage in life in sexual experience, with many similarities to and sensations of the very early instinctual pattern.)

Mother's presence

This infant has been introduced into the world and a terrifying array of passions in a very short space of time. From day one, a baby has to assuage his raging hunger, and in this the mother plays an integral part. When he is very tiny, a baby's world consists only of himself, in all his totally helpless vulnerability. All his comfort and pain seem to originate from within himself. The whole outside world, including his mother, seems to be an extension of himself. He cries, and someone will come to attend to him; the ability to suck a comforting thumb reinforces his fantasy that he can manage everything from within himself. Before long, however, the baby is confronted by the difficult business of distinguishing the reality from the fantasy and discovering what is 'me' and what is 'not me'. He finds that he cannot control mother absolutely; when he is in the middle of doing some-thing together with her, the phone rings or one of the other children requires urgent attention. This is all exceedingly frustrating!

So, in addition to the pangs of hunger, a baby has to cope with a confusion of conflicting feelings. For the first year or so, the baby's ability to handle the strong feelings aroused by these experiences is very limited. In the early months, the mother's task is to reduce unnecessary agitation as much as possible, and, by her reassuring presence, to help the baby to bear what cannot be avoided.

As well as trying to reduce frustration, the mother will also be helping the baby to bring together both the periods of intense excitement and the rest periods in between, when nothing much is happening but when there is warmth, security and protection from the unpredictable. These periods of quietness are as important as the exciting periods; times when the baby is just lying quietly or playing alone, knowing that mother is around, and times when mother and baby are playing their own little games together. The child who is subjected to endless stimulation from some person outside himself will never have a chance to discover the riches that lie waiting within himself and will always be dependent on the outside world to provide the entertainment. (This may produce difficulties for him when he is older!) But unless the baby is developing a secure and adequate relationship with his mother, he will not be able to be content and at home within himself.

Freud called the first year the 'oral phase', because the baby's mouth is the area of which the baby is most aware. Not only does the satisfying food go in there, but everything else as well, including fists, fingers, other people's fingers, teddy's ears, plastic rings, bits of cloth and everything which can be handled. Moreover, delicious bubbling sensations and noises can be made with the mouth. The mouth is the primary medium for exploring the world and providing excitement. Oral satisfactions die hard. Adults eat to ease depression, turn to the bottle for comfort, or suck contentedly on a pipe. All these habits have a link with babyhood experiences.

The child has been created and is now being sustained by the intimate care of the parents. Already they are in the place of God for this child before he knows anything about it intellectually. There seem to be shades of Joseph Addison's old hymn here:

> Unnumbered comforts to my soul
> Thy tender care bestowed;

40

Before my infant heart conceived
From whom these comforts flowed.[1]

Mother's absence

The baby's mother is there not just to see that he does
not starve physically, or fall into the fire. If the infant
does not have the emotional presence of his mother (or
some *constant, known, and reliable* mother-substitute) to
mediate and moderate the experiences of life for him,
he has to defend himself somehow from the intense
anxiety her absence produces. (Her absence need not
be physical; she may be in the vicinity, but emotionally
unavailable.) The child will do this by withdrawing
into a world of his own where he does not feel pain;
nor does he feel love or the desire to reach out and
make contact with other people. Alternatively, he may
become very demanding and manipulative. Of course,
children are amazingly resilient and most of them
devise means of surviving somehow, but at the same
time as they are surviving, they are also having to deal
with the hidden feelings which the absence of a secure
base promotes. If, in an extreme case, the child is left,
consistently, to scream unattended for longer than he
can tolerate (which is not long in adult terms), he is
pushed into 'dread, disintegration, death of the self,
and nothingness', to quote Dr Frank Lake.[2] This has
profound implications for the person's view of himself
and the business of relating to other people and their
expectations.

The healthy growing baby

One of my teachers, the late Dr Donald Winnicott,
coined the phrase 'the good-enough mother' to describe, not a perfect mother, but one who is 'good

enough' to make life a reasonably comfortable experience and who can provide an environment in which the child can make sense of himself and of the world. In this chapter we have looked, very briefly, at some of the ways in which a baby grows emotionally while growing physically. We have traced the outlines of the good-enough environment which facilitates healthy growth. The good-enough response to physical and emotional needs enables this baby to feel like a living entity in his or her own right. An unself-conscious, solid self-esteem is growing: 'It's all right to be me: I enjoy being me – most of the time.' It cannot be stated too often that the quality of the child's first human relationship is the foundation-stone of his personality, on which the whole edifice rests.

A child's tie to his mother

In his book entitled *Attachment*,[3] Dr John Bowlby examines the nature of the mysterious tie that exists between mother and child. He draws attention to mother birds and animals with their young, such a familiar sight in the spring: a flotilla of ducklings scurrying after their mother duck; swans and cygnets gliding downstream; ewes and lambs; cows and calves in the fields. We know that human children follow their mother about in much the same way. It is such a universal phenomenon that people rarely stop to ask what it is about.

In many species the young are born in a sufficiently advanced state of development for them to move about independently within a few hours of birth. In those cases, when the mother sets off in any direction, the young will follow automatically. The instinct to follow is so ingrained that a duckling has been known to follow the first thing that moved, be it a cardboard box or a human being.

In other species, including carnivores and rodents, the development of the newborn is much less advanced. Weeks or even months elapse before the young are able to move about on their own, but once they can do so the tendency is to keep close to the mother. Almost immediately after birth, all primate infants cling to their mother, and if they are not able to sustain their own weight they are assisted by their mother. All through early childhood they are either in direct physical contact with her or very near her. As they grow older, the amount of direct contact decreases and they wander farther off. But at the first sign of alarm they rush back, and at night they sleep with her. The tendency to keep near to the mother is apparent.

There are two main characteristics of this behaviour: first the need to maintain proximity, and secondly, the attachment between the particular mother and the particular offspring concerned. Any other mother or offspring is frequently rejected. The parent and the young behave towards each other very differently from the ways in which they behave to all others of the same species. Dr Bowlby refers to the behaviour of the young as *attachment behaviour* and to the behaviour of the parent as *care-taking behaviour*. As the young get older, they spend less time with the mother and more with peers and other adults. This change is mainly the result of their own initiative.

Attachment behaviour takes much longer to appear in human babies than in many animal species or sub-human primates. In unsophisticated human societies the infant is carried by the mother on her back and kept in close proximity all the time. Only in more 'advanced' human societies is the baby left in a pram or cot, out of contact with his or her mother for many hours of the day and often during the night.

The establishment of *trust*

By the time they are about four months old, infants in a good-enough family setting will be responding to their mother differently from the way in which they respond to other people. They will smile and gurgle at her more readily and follow her with their eyes for longer. They will cry when she leaves the room and proximity is interrupted. This attachment behaviour 'grows more vigorous and regular as though the attachment to the mother is becoming stronger and more consolidated',[4] and it continues until about the middle of the fourth year. The purpose of this attachment behaviour is to ensure the protection of the offspring – both physical and emotional protection.

If the mother rebuffs the child or is inattentive to him, the child's behaviour becomes much more clinging (remember the child in the supermarket in chapter 1?); but the more he feels he is the centre of her stage, so to speak, the more he will feel confident enough to let her go, gradually. Research[5] demonstrates that, generally, about a month after the sample of children studied had first shown attachment behaviour, a quarter of them were directing it to other members of the family; and by the time they had reached eighteen months, all but a handful of the children were attached to at least one other figure, and often to several. After the mother, the father was the one who most frequently elicited the attachment behaviour; then came the older children who might from time to time be the care-takers, but it was also directed to pre-school children. The researchers found no evidence that attachment to the mother became less intense when attachment behaviour was directed towards other people as well. On the contrary, in the early months of attachment, the greater the number of people to whom a child was attached, the more intense was his attachment to the mother as the primary carer. But, in any one child the intensity and consistency with which the attachment behaviour was shown could vary greatly from day to day or hour to hour.

There is abundant evidence that, although the quality of care an infant receives plays a major part in attachment behaviour, the infant himself initiates and influences the interaction to a large and surprisingly powerful extent by his gurgles, smiles, movements and cries. Sister Frances Dominica, who runs the Helen House hospice for children in Oxford, had taken into her personal care a Ghanaian baby boy and had become his legal guardian. She was considering his future. Adoption? Fostering? But one of the things that she had not taken into account was

the fact that even a tiny child is going to put an immense amount of energy from *his* side into bonding, so that within two days I was feeling this *incredibly* strong energy from him. I had naïvely thought, if I'd thought about it all, that it would be the adult who would start building the relationship, and it's not actually: it's the child. I've talked to a lot of parents since, and they confirmed what I experienced. It's amazing.[6]

During this initial stage of development, the infant is laying the foundation of every subsequent relationship – *trust and love*. The ability to trust is built into his emotional bloodstream by the constant and repeated experience that the adults in his life (particularly the mother) relate and respond to his emotional and physical needs, and are reliable and 'good enough'. And he begins to understand about mutual love because they first loved him (compare 1 Jn. 4:19).

Separation

Wendy was grown up when her mother told her: 'You used to lie in your cot crying and crying. I never knew what was the matter with you. You weren't hungry or ill, you weren't wet, dirty or cold, and there were no pins sticking in you. There was nothing wrong with you, but you wouldn't stop crying. You stopped as soon as I picked you up. I used to feel like throwing you out of the window!'

Wendy's mother did not understand about getting to *know* her baby: she did not understand that from the baby's point of view there was something very wrong. The mother thought that physical care was all that was necessary, and that if the external conditions were right everything else would look after itself. She did not understand that this tiny person was very distressed about something or other, so she just put it down to 'badness'.

It was years later that Wendy made the connection. She was only six weeks old when her mother was admitted to hospital (where she stayed for ten days) for treatment for a breast abscess. As far as baby Wendy was concerned, this separation was a total tearing in this rudimentary relationship, unexpected and inexplicable. Her mother was suddenly absent. She had no means of understanding why she had been 'abandoned'. The voice, the smell, the touch, the eyes, the warm breasts, were no longer there. Wendy was left high and dry.

Her distracted father was deputed to look after her, but he had not the slightest idea what to do, and in any case his touch and smell were different and he had no warm breasts. Suddenly there was a bottle, which was a very different proposition from the breast. Wendy's little world had collapsed. An aunt, who had never seen Wendy before, came to the rescue; but this woman was just as strange as her father. No doubt they did their best, but babies are very sensitive to atmosphere and Wendy must have picked up some of the agitation. It is conceivable that the previous feed-times had become a bit difficult before her mother's departure, and Wendy may have sensed some wincing and reluctance instead of the former generous supply of lovely milk. Babies cannot cope with things for long, and ten days is an eternity. When her mother eventually reappeared, Wendy did not know her. The subsequent crying may very well have been connected with this incident of total trauma for Wendy, when the 'getting to know you' process was so cruelly disrupted and she was left with nothing to 'hold' her inner needs. Wendy needed her mother absolutely.

As an adult, one of Wendy's methods of survival was to be obstrusively vivacious and sparkling. She was noisy, ebullient and 'always taking responsibility for other people's business'. She herself used to grow very tired of this, but could not find another way of 'feeling alive'. She used to have distressing dreams which bore veiled references to her early trauma. It was as though she were responsible for feeding her own inner needs, and, if she did not, nobody else would. Her favourite pastime was to search for some unusual and very beautiful garment or special material. She would not wear whatever she had

47

bought; it was the search itself which was so absorbing. It took a long time for her to realize that she was still searching for the precious thing that she had lost so long ago, now represented by soft, beautiful material. (As we know well, little children comfort themselves with their own thumbs, furry objects or soft pieces of cloth, as they gradually experience the inevitable distancing from the mother.)

The next layer of building-bricks: *autonomy*

Time moves on and, before we know it, our baby is achieving some sort of independence. He gradually makes the astonishing discovery that he can sit up unsupported and that he can shuffle from one place to another under his own steam. This is excitement indeed! And it gets even more heady when he can support himself on his wobbly legs and take a staggering step or two. All that kicking in the pram has not been for nothing, after all! The world is there for him to explore. He can put his shoes in the fridge; he can pull the cloth hanging over the edge of the table, with the ensuing lovely and unexpected cascade of noisy crockery. And he falls down from time to time. He may not hurt himself, but if someone does not come at once to reassure him, he will start to cry to ensure that they know about it. If he is badly hurt or shocked, only his mother's presence will do. Our baby is moving into the second major phase of his development and building on the basic foundation layer.

As the child grows into the first and second year, the parents will be helping him to incorporate the different varieties of experience which befall him. At the same time they will be trying to make sure that the sense of security is not undermined. The child can tolerate frustration only if there is sufficient compensatory satisfaction and nourishment.

He has established the sense of trust. As his horizons widen because of increased locomotion and perception, he is now beginning to establish the sense of his own personal *autonomy*. He has, to some extent, control over his own body, and is no longer the largely helpless recipient of other people's decisions. Every day brings some new discovery about his increasing capacity; not only about physical accomplishments ('Me do it!'), but also the exciting new capacity to say, 'No, don't want to!'

One of the great personal achievements at this stage is the control of bladder and bowel (hence the fact that Freud called this the 'anal' phase). This is an important stage of progress in its own right, but it also indicates a greater degree of social co-operation and a widening capacity fo relate to the outside world. A child who has had a fairly satisfactory relationship during the feeding stage will usually be able to go through this one relatively quietly. Unless there is some organic problem, the smooth physical functioning of a child will be in tandem with the smooth emotional development. There will be no need for him to practise regular withholding of the things which seem to interest his mother so much. But, if there is some trauma, such as the arrival of a new baby, or a prolonged separation from mother, or great unhappiness in the general atmosphere, it is not unusual for the child to regress to the previous stage of development as a result of the anxiety which he experiences. The new-found independence is abandoned in favour of bottles, nappies and thumb-sucking. It is possible to move on adequately to the next phase only when the current one has been satisfactorily accomplished, and often there is some oscillation between the two.

It is vital for this little person to receive encouragement and affirmation in the first faltering effort to discover the boundaries. Great patience is required by the adults, to afford the child enough time and space to do what he is trying to do, and to appreciate the often messy result of 'Me do it!' All this loving and patient care is a reflection of the parent side of God.

> It was I who taught [my people] to walk,
>   taking them by the arms . . .
> I led them with cords of human kindness,
>   with ties of love;
> I lifted the yoke from their neck
>   and bent down to feed them.
>   (Ho. 11:3–4)

5

Separation, positive and negative

Kerry was an average nine-month-old when her mother went back to work part-time as a teacher. She had made arrangements for Kerry to be looked after by a friend who was fairly familiar to her. This arrangement worked quite well because it applied for only two half-days a week and Kerry slept for much of that time. As she grew older, however, the times away from her mother gradually increased and Kerry slept less. Her child-minder described her as 'very well behaved – better than my own children'.

But it was noticeable, as she went out in the buggy, that she was unusually passive; she did not respond to the greetings of passers-by, seldom smiled and rarely spoke. She even preferred to ride in the buggy rather than walk. Her appetite was tiny and she often had difficulty in the toilet. When her mother came to collect her, she would break out into noise and talk; but she often clung to the child-minder, refusing to go home with her mother. She also called the child-minder 'Mum' very frequently. Not surprisingly, Kerry's mother was upset by these reactions, not realizing that this little girl was being asked to encompass something that was beyond her skills. Now, three years later, Kerry is at school full-time herself. She is still collected by the same child-minder quite often, but her behaviour is much more aggressive; she disturbs the play of the other children as soon as her mother comes into sight, and tries all sorts of attention-attracting tactics.

Kerry is just a normal little girl, reacting in a way we might expect to the situation in which she finds herself. Her child-minder says that in her opinion the experience of partial separation from her mother has not been helpful in Kerry's development.

If a very young baby has to go into a day nursery, it is usually a separation situation of some perplexity for that child. The carers will probably be loving and attentive people, but from the baby's-eye view they are an assortment of people with whom it is seldom possible to make that vital one-to-one relationship. Every time he needs attention a different person comes, and different faces peer over the cot to smile at him and talk to him. What is this baby to do as he looks urgently into his tiny heart and limited experience for a stable relationship? He will survive, of course. He will learn to play and achieve things. But he may very well be learning, also, not to commit himself to anyone on a deep level because no-one is ultimately committed to him on that level, as far as his heart tells him. Not a good omen for future relationships! There are already enough people around who cannot commit themselves to anyone or anything for a sustained period.

Obviously, from the child's point of view he is better off in his own familiar surroundings with the people he knows; but there are, of course, occasions when for one reason or another it is necessary for him to be put into a day nursery or with a child-minder. Each child reacts differently to this separation. After the age of two, they can usually cope with it reasonably well, provided the alternative care-taking is of a good, personal quality and that the child's home is a stable and loving environment.

If the child goes to nursery school, he may be quite upset initially when the mother is about to leave. He may cry angrily in protest or painfully in grief, and when he stops he will remain silent and inactive or become very demanding, probably in marked contrast to the way in which he would behave if his mother were there.

When children reach their fourth year, however, they usually adjust much better to their mother's temporary absence because they have acquired a little experience on which to build. They play with other children, provided that the people caring for them are in some way associated in their mind with their mother; that they are in good health and not in a state of alarm; that they know where their mother is and that they can resume contact with her at short notice. If any of these conditions does not operate, the child is likely to be very 'mummyish', or to show other behaviour disturbances.

The child uses his mother as a base from which to explore, but that can only be done if he feels safe emotionally with that secure base.

The years between one and two mark the stage when the child is just beginning to separate a little from mother on his own initiative. It is vital for this to happen, and for mother to let it happen when the time comes, spontaneously and to the extent that the child can manage. If there is too much clinging by either child or mother, the child will become stuck in the developmental processes (for instance, he will not be able to be at all independent, or to make little decisions, or to tolerate being apart), to the great detriment of both. Increasingly, attachment behaviour subsides; but children of five, six and seven (and older) sometimes like a cuddle, or if something goes wrong at school or with friends, they want to return at once to the parent or parent-substitute.

The last foundational building-bricks: *identity*

Until a child is about three, he sees another child as just another child; but now he is gradually developing the ability to play co-operatively with this other child. Now he knows who he is in his own right.

But another gradual change is becoming apparent. This is the increasing awareness of the difference between 'girl' and 'boy'. The growing child begins to know to which gender he or she belongs. There is also an increasingly clear awareness that his or her parents are similar but different on many levels. The way in which the child relates to one parent will begin to include differences from the way in which he or she relates to the other. In the to-ing and fro-ing of family interaction, the child's own gender identity becomes established.

During the years from three to six it is absolutely vital for a growing child to live with two parents of the opposite sex who love each other openly and at times exclude the child from their lives. It is hard for the child; no-one likes being excluded from the fun, but this is another separation stepping-stone. Until now, this child has seen himself or herself as mother's priority commitment. Now, he or she is having to learn that Dad got there first. The little boy has to begin to withdraw his identification from his mother and transfer it to his father. In his ambivalence and struggle he will make comments like, 'When I grow up I'm going to marry Mummy', or 'We don't need Daddy, do we?' The little girl has a slightly easier time, in that she can continue to identify with her mother as being the object of her father's love.

A. A. Milne understood the way a child sees life.

He set out some of the aspects of omnipotence, separation, modelling and possessiveness in his poem:

James James
Morrison Morrison
Wetherby George Du Pree
Took great care of his Mother
Though he was only three.
James James
Said to his Mother
'Mother,' he said, said he,
'You must never go down to the end of the town
   if you don't go down with me.'

James James
Morrison's Mother
Put on a golden gown.
James James
Morrison's Mother
Drove to the end of town.
James James
Morrison's Mother
Said to herself, said she,
'I can get right down to the end of the town
   and be back in time for tea.'

King James
Put up a notice:
'LOST, or STOLEN or STRAYED!
JAMES JAMES
MORRISON'S MOTHER
SEEMS TO HAVE BEEN MISLAID.
LAST SEEN WANDERING VAGUELY:
QUITE OF HER OWN ACCORD
SHE TRIED TO GET DOWN TO THE END OF
   THE TOWN.
FORTY SHILLINGS REWARD!'

James James
Morrison Morrison
(Commonly known as Jim)
Told his other relations
Not to go blaming *him*.
James James
Said to his Mother
'Mother,' he said, said he,
'You must *never* go down to the end of the town
    without consulting me.'

James James
Morrison's Mother
Hasn't been heard of since.
King John said he was sorry;
So did the Queen and Prince.
King John
(Somebody told me)
Said to a man he knew:
'If people go down to the end of the town,
    well what can *anyone* do?'

James James
M. M.
W. G. Du P.
Took great
C/o his M*****
Though he was only three.
J. J.
Said to his M*****
'M*****,' he said, said he,
'You-must-never-go-down-to-the-end-of-the-
    town-if-you-don't-go-down-with-ME.'

It is easy to see that in a one-parent family, or
where the parents do not love each other, this stage

of development becomes very confused indeed for the child. His or her sexual development and identity can become blurred and the perception of the way men and women relate to each other is inevitably impaired. This usually has serious repercussions on his or her later relationships, sexual orientation, expectations and attitudes to marriage.

This is the time when great questions are asked: 'Where did I come from?' and 'Why wasn't I on your wedding photos?' Fascination with genital and erotic areas of life is expanding. This is Freud's 'genital phase'. Before the deadening influence of television and computers, children used to play out their fantasies about their inner world in games of 'Mummies and Daddies' and hospitals and doctors. Even now, adults are treated to (what seem to the children as uproarious) lavatorial jokes which are all in the general area of genitalia and about producing things from one's own body. (Some adults are still stuck at this point, it seems!)

Imagine the damage to a growing child when he or she is subjected to sexual abuse and introduced inappropriately to adult sexual activity at a time when so many other things are developing in the child's life. This is a very serious issue and an immensely damaging activity which can have ruinous effects. It is such an important subject in its own right that here I can only refer readers to some of the books available.[1]

The latency period

Up to the age of about six, our child has been having to absorb a dazzling array of emotional experiences – love, hate, envy, anxiety, tenderness, vulnerability, jealousy, success, failure, pain, learning to share –

and more. He knows who he is as a separate individual and the foundations of personality have been laid. The next few years are spent in consolidation and physical growth, testing and retesting the limits, abilities and boundaries. These boundaries also include understanding about the appropriateness of behaviour, which some adults would call 'conscience'.

The onset of adolescence stirs up all these stages again. 'Where do I belong?' 'What can I do and where are the limits?' 'What is this big sex thing about?' The difference is that an adolescent is more potent than a child in more ways than one.

Planting the time bomb

Involuntary separation and loss over a long period are potentially traumatic during all the years of infancy, childhood and adolescence. Separation from parents cuts into the roots of a child's existence because he feels them to be such an integral part of his life. Not surprisingly, if they withdraw for any reason, he feels confused and disorientated. Many a child who has been sent to boarding-school at too early an age, or when his emotional security was not firm enough, has told of the damage this does in forming close attachments in later life.

This involuntary separation is one of the worst experiences that can occur to a growing child. If known and trusted parent-substitutes are readily available, the trauma may be mitigated to some extent, and made more manageable. But since the child is still at the stage of believing himself to be the centre around which the world revolves, there is the inevitable sense that the child himself must have been the cause of the separation in some way. The cause usually settles on the fact that he himself is so unlovable and 'bad', and that all the naughty thoughts and wishes that have crossed his mind have become a reality. So there is an indefinable sense of guilt, responsibility and confusion. There is also a terrible sense of trust having been broken, and it does not mend easily.

It is very important for us to try to understand something of the emotional life of a small child so that we can see how vital it is for him to be growing up in a united, loving and committed family. We can then try to avoid planting time bombs.

Foundations are under the ground. They are not seen by onlookers. What the onlookers see is the building which rests upon those foundations; but the whole superstructure rests upon that hidden part. Sometimes there is damage to an upper wall or floor; this can be a nuisance and may require inconvenient repair. But if there is a foundational flaw, the repair operation is much more difficult, complicated and extensive, and sometimes impossible. When we are thinking about human beings in terms of buildings, we can see that some external assault by the slings and arrows of outrageous fortune (such as bereavement) may disturb the visible fabric. The person may need some help, which may vary from friendly support to pastoral counselling of some sort. But when we are looking at some fundamental personality difficulty (for example, persistent depression, chronic low self-esteem, inability to make satisfactory relationships, irrational fears and inexplicable obsessions), it may be that therapy of a much more radical nature would be helpful as another aspect of the ministry of the Holy Spirit. This would involve uncovering and rebuilding some of the foundations at the point where development was interrupted. All levels of help are valid if they are applied appropriately to the need and if they help the individual to find himself, and thus to be responsible for his own attitudes and behaviour.

A life-long process

All life is full of painful separations and 'little deaths'. Already in two years or so, the child has discovered this; first at birth, then in the process of developing his own autonomy. One thing has to go before another can take its place. But the one thing can be let go satisfactorily only if the new thing holds some purpose or creates motivation. If the new thing seems too painful or pointless, the old thing is hard to relinquish. So, when the future seems unwelcome and difficult, the little child (and adults) will baulk at change and make every effort to keep things as they are.

The life-long need

Throughout babyhood, attachment behaviour is paramount; throughout the latency period between the ages of about six and puberty it is dominant; during adolescence it remains strong, but powerful attachments to other people develop. The quality of our first experiences of it will often determine how well we can give or receive this attachment behaviour subsequently. For everyone, attachment to parents (or lack of it) continues into adult life and influences behaviour in countless ways. As adults, we still need attachments for comfort and protection, and in times of trouble, sorrow, need, sickness or any other adversity we will almost certainly seek proximity to, and the 'presence' of, some known and trusted person.

('Presence' means more than just physical proximity: it is the sense of being encompassed in the love of someone.) In his moving book *An Evil Cradling*, Brian Keenan recalls that amid the unspeakable experiences in his Beirut captivity, 'At times God seemed so real and so intimately close . . . In its own way our isolation had expanded the heart, not to reach out to a detached God but to find and become part of whatever "God" might be.'[2]

Even our Lord Jesus needed his friends to watch and pray with him at his hour of supreme agony and approaching death. And at the last, it is most important that, if possible, we should not be left alone when the time of death comes. Attachment behaviour plays a vital role from the cradle to the grave. However adult we are, we always have something of the vulnerable child within us – otherwise we would be inhuman.

6

The 'good-enough' mother

What is a mother? What a stupid question! Everyone knows what a mother is! Or do they?

I turned to the *Shorter Oxford Dictionary* (two huge volumes of it) and found a variety of informative definitions of 'mother'. Among them were: 1. a female parent; 2. a woman who has given birth to a child; 3. a woman who exercises control like that of a mother; 4. a term of address for an elderly woman of the lower classes; 5. a ropy mucilaginous substance produced in vinegar during acetous fermentation by a mould-fungus. So now we know what a mother is!

Andrew, aged seventeen, would agree with definition 5 as a description of his mother. 'She's a right pain in the neck, sometimes!' (Andrew's mother could return the compliment from time to time, with a certain amount of vehemence!) He is tall, too handsome for his own good, the product of an excellent school and just about to do his 'A' levels prior to naval training at Dartmouth, which has been his long-standing ambition. Incidentally, his mother had continued her career outside the home, as well as working within it, with the main intention of contributing to the heavy costs of the education that Andrew's parents considered would be the best for his particular temperament. 'She nags me something awful about the way I spend money or the fact that I get behind with my school work. She gets on my wick, sometimes.' But he also said, 'She is the one who puts her foot down. I used to think she just did it to annoy me, but I realize now that she did it for my good, and I suppose it is really part of her love for me. She has done a lot for me, really.'

People in the outside world can see that one of the reasons why Andrew has the makings of a solid citizen is that his mother has always been available for him emotionally, has 'held' the periodic outbursts of intense feeling throughout his life, and has helped him to establish limits and realistic goals for himself, both when he was very small and now that he is almost an adult. But it has not always been an easy ride for Andrew or his mother.

The importance of the earliest days

Nowadays there is much awareness of the lasting impact of childhood experiences: we hear about it from all quarters. Not that it is such a very new concept. Thousands of years ago the wise King Solomon said: 'Train a child in the way he should go, and when he is old he will not turn from it' (Pr. 22:6). And Wordsworth's line, 'The child is father of the man,' is well known. The Jesuits have said for years, 'Give me a child until it is seven and I have it for the rest of its life.'

Those early, impressionable days are indeed vital. The virgin soil of early childhood bears the permanent imprint of its environment and experiences. There is no previous history on which the child can call as a mitigating or balancing factor. Although the small child has no perception of dependence, there is probably no other point in his life when the child will be so utterly dependent on every level, unless he is unfortunate enough to experience the indignity of 'second childhood'. The difference between these two stages is that the dependence of infancy is accepted as normal and usually elicits loving care and tenderness, whereas the dependence of old age is often regarded as burdensome and sometimes elicits rejection.

The task of the mother

It is very important for us to know what is happening in the *inner* world of a child. If you acquire a plant for your garden, you must investigate what sort of soil it likes, whether it needs much or little sunshine and water, and so on. You don't just buy something because your friend has a nice one, stick it in the ground and expect it to blossom, regardless. Or maybe some of us do, and then wonder why it turns out to be such a disappointment! Of course, some plants are resilient and will tolerate almost any sort of treatment or neglect. Others are delicate and require special attention, protection and food. Pruning, tying back and dividing are necessary from time to time, as well as tender loving care of the right sort for the individual plant's needs to ensure the best growth.

In the same way, children have their own natural urge towards life and their particular inherent tendencies which we call 'personality'. It is the task of the adults who care for them to understand and co-operate with each individual's particular way of developing. This requires a great deal of adaptation and commitment on the part of the parents and, initially, of the mother especially. Children are not just pieces of clay which need to be moulded.

One young mother hates attending functions at her husband's firm. 'People come up to you all brightly and ask what you do. "Oh, I'm just a housewife and mother," I reply. Then they just say "Oh!" which means "How boring!" and I feel totally stupid, like a fish out of water. It makes you feel such a fool. All these career women look so smart and attractive. They lead stimulating lives and can make intelligent conversation. All I seem to know about is that Tommy has lost his pencil and Susan fell down at school. My world seems so narrow. They make me feel completely unadventurous and stupid, as though they think I have nothing to do at home because I don't "work". That's a joke!'

Yet motherhood is the most demanding and important career there is, even if it is not the most glamorous. 'Everyone tells you how wonderful it is going to be, to have this lovely baby which everyone will admire. No-one tells you how tired you will get and what a struggle it will sometimes be to cope with the boredom and drudgery and still be unselfish, understanding and adaptable.' Not every woman is automatically and naturally outgoing and loving towards her child; for some it takes time, and others will never be 'motherly' people. In our culture we have tended to equate 'woman' with 'mother' to an unrealistic extent.

Is it not strange, therefore, that for such an influential career there is no training? And strange, too, that such a tremendously important task should depend so little on a high intelligence quotient? This may well be because, at root, mothering is about relationship and love, not about intellectual capacity or cerebral knowledge.

The essential requisite

The essential requisite is the capacity to know how the baby is feeling and how to respond appropriately; for the mother to be able to receive, absorb and digest all the horrible feelings of the baby (fury, fear, general unnamed distress, *etc.*), and return them in a manageable form. This 'holding' can be done by someone who has no intellectual knowledge of what is happening in the relationship between the mother and the baby, but who has a great intuitive sense of it. That is difficult to teach!

If the mother is so exasperated by the demands of the baby that she shouts and screams at him and sometimes hits him, it is a very terrifying experience for the baby. The baby's own feelings of fury are bad enough to have to endure without having his mother's as well. The mother has, somehow, to be able to hold the baby's powerful feelings and thereby make them safe so that the baby can eventually tolerate them. Most mothers will have experienced times of exasperation when it is hard to do this and will be tempted to envy the idealized lives of the nine-to-five women! It is immensely difficult to rise above one's own impulses of anger when the scream-ing baby has just gone too far. The angry mother and the angry baby intensify each other's frustration.

This is where another person's presence is impor-tant to hold the mother, so that she can hold the baby more calmly. It is very necessary for the mother to have times when she herself can be held either by her husband, or by having some time to herself so that, on the whole, she can retain her calmness.

If the mother is not there to hold and mediate these disturbing emotions, the child has to do it for himself. In this case the child learns, too early, to become independent. He may well become the sort of person who, in adult life, always operates in overdrive and is afraid of inner stillness, because that means that there is nothing there – no-one to deflect the pain, anxiety and fear. So he has to create something to fill the fearful emptiness, to control it and keep it at a distance.

The baby's-eye view

The mother's most important task is not so much to keep the baby clean and well fed – though this is obviously important – as to *understand the baby's language*. This is specially so during the first few months. The pleasure that the mother gets from all the things involved in the care of the infant (the temperature of the bath water, the smell of a clean baby, the feel of the clothes) are all important to the baby, but the mother's *presence* and her enjoyment are what the baby needs most. Whatever is important to the mother is important to the baby, and vice versa. There is something inside most mothers which recognizes and knows how to respond to the baby's non-verbal language after a while. She has a special ability to put herself in the place of the infant and so to know how the infant is feeling. (This ability recedes after a few months.) If the mother feels unselfconsciously at ease within herself, she will trust her own inner wisdom and need not rely heavily on books or the instructions of other people She may have been fortunate enough to have watched her own mother or friends dealing with younger brothers and sisters, and she may have practised on her own dolls, thereby acquiring some practical skills and understanding.

But the main ingredient is love. Love means commitment, not sentimentality. Love is fairly basic; it involves all sorts of things which may seem at first sight to be in opposition – patience and impatience, generosity and limitations, power and humility, toughness and tenderness.

The basis of the bond

This specially intimate love is the basis of the bonding between mother and baby. It has been said that there is no such thing as a baby; it is always a case of 'mother and baby'. The baby cannot exist without the mother, and the mother's life centres round the baby, at least for the first few months. The mother may be devoted to her baby, but the only way a baby can understand this is that *she* (not a substitute) is usually there when he calls; that she is committed to the baby through thick and thin, regardless of the cost to herself, of which the baby is totally unaware. 'Over and over again a mother deals with her own moods, anxieties and excitements in her own private life, reserving for her baby what belongs to the baby.'[1]

Other people can keep him clean, but no-one else will have that very intimate and special bond with him which holds him emotionally. The aim of infant care is not merely to establish a physically healthy individual; it is to include the richest possible experience of relationship which will have long-term effects on the personality and character of that infant. If the emotional bonding is defective, this will soon be reflected in the baby's physical state and general restlessness.

The 'good-enough' environment

While the baby is growing inside the mother, the two of them are getting to know one another, physically and emotionally. They share the same joys and sorrows, the same meals, the same drugs, alcohol, coffee, nicotine and the same air. The foetus is affected by the mother's emotions and activities or relaxation. Mother and baby are bound together and the foetus is affected by everything that the mother experiences. The mother becomes increasingly preoccupied with what is going on inside her, both physically and emotionally. She needs to be given space to 'commune' with the unborn infant and her own state of 'maternal preoccupation' in preparation for what is to come. Maternal preoccupation reflects a particular relationship of one mother with one child.

After the baby is born, the mother and baby will forge an even closer relationship, both while the infant lies quietly in his cot, holding his mother's finger and gazing at her face, and also in the excitement of feed-times, when his hands touch her skin and he smells her body and his desperate hunger begins to be appeased. Obviously, breast-feeding brings the baby and mother into the most intimate contact with each other. Theories about the respective values of breast and bottle go in and out of fashion. Nowadays, the breast is in vogue as being healthier from a phsyical point of view. But the important factors are the intimacy of the situation, and the fact that it is something which only the mother and baby can do for each other. The baby will be looking at her and 'taking her in' in more ways than one. In this world full of strange, new experiences, he will hear the well-known and reassuring sound of the mother's heartbeat. He will be getting to know her in a different way from before – her voice, her touch, her eyes, the taste of her, and her familiar smell. He will begin to respond to this constant and repeated experience of enjoyment, comfort and love, through the use of his five senses. The mother's and baby's primary task is to get to know each other because of the satisfaction and relief it brings to both of them.

The mother's role is to *do* something for her baby, but her essence is to *be* something for that baby. 'I am' always comes before 'I do', in mothering as in everything else. People often talk about a woman's *role*, but do not pay much attention to her *essence*.

In her book *Woman's Mysteries*, Esther Harding, a Jungian analyst, has drawn attention to the typical problem of the modern woman, who, owing to the increasing development of her masculine side, is in danger of losing touch with the instinctive roots of her being. Harding says that this inevitable conflict between the masculine and feminine elements which characterizes the situation of the woman in the Western world (and of the professional woman in particular) is rarely, if ever, experienced consciously and particularly by her. Both by nature and inclination, women in general tend to avoid specific consciousness and painfulness in conflict. The woman usually identifies with one side or the other (that is, with her feminine or her masculine element), rather than wrestling with the conflict.[2]

Maternal preoccupation

During these very early months the new mother, in

her maternal preoccupation, needs to be protected from too much intrusion from the outside world, because motherhood is highly demanding. This protection may come from the extended family, friends and certainly from the father of the child. Motherhood, at any stage, but particularly in the first months, does not thrive on poverty, poor housing or an unhappy marriage. Nor can it flourish with ease when there is a history of emotional deprivation or mental instability. The mother is already engaged on a task of great magnitude and sensitivity, and if she is distracted by too many external worries or engagements she cannot be at liberty to attend to the most important task on hand, that of growing another human being.

The world of the tiny baby exists within the orbit of a one-to-one relationship with his mother. In her he lives and moves and has his being. Without her, he is lost and frightened. A *consistent and committed* mother-substitute can fulfil a very adequate function, provided that she is there on call most of the time, day and night, and has grown to understand and anticipate the baby's expressions, noises and movements, which are the baby's language.

A little group of Chinese were sitting in Heathrow Airport awaiting their flight's departure to Hong Kong. There were several adults of various ages and one small girl aged about a year. She was such a good little thing, like a little doll, with her dark eyes and black hair cut in a straight front and sides. She was staggering about between the adults, who were playing with her in turns. Then came the inevitable moment when she tripped over someone's feet and lay flat on the floor for a silent minute. She had not hurt herself, but she obviously felt dislodged in some way. Then came the whimpering, so her father

71

picked her up and talked to her. She would not be comforted, so she was passed to someone else. But that would not do, either. By this time the cries were becoming a bit frantic. Then, fortunately, her mother arrived; she had been to the duty-free shop or somewhere for a break. She took the child in her arms – and instantly there was calm. Emotional safety was re-established and in a few moments the child was toddling about again. The baby's-eye view is the same in whatever culture they belong.

The 'facilitating environment'

A 'facilitating environment' starts with a high degree of adaptation on the part of the mother to the individual needs of the baby. Dr Winnicott wrote:

> As she begins to get to know the infant, she can help him or her to encompass the new and frightening transition from contentment whether asleep or awake, to the raging attack of the hungry lions within ... The messy business of the care of a newborn infant is a full-time job and one which can be done well by only one person in the richness of the continuous hour-by-hour contact with the baby.[3]

This is essential to an increased understanding of the baby's language. Within this atmosphere the baby receives 'good-enough' mothering, especially if the feeding process, with all its emotional overtones, is going well. This baby and this mother will together be laying down some firm foundations for later development of personality.

The vital importance of the nurturing quality of the

relationship between mother and small child cannot be over-emphasized. In view of all this, Dr Winnicott, who spent all his professional life observing and treating children and their mothers, concluded:

> For my part I am sure that while mothercraft may be taught and even read about in books, the mothering of one's own baby is entirely personal, a job that no one else could take over and do as well as oneself . . . This opinion, I may as well add, is not based on hearing mothers talk, on guess-work, or on pure intuition: it is the conclusion I feel I have been forced to draw after long research.[4]

This is the sort of situation we are reminded of repeatedly in David's psalms. How many times did he bewail the fact that the Lord had hidden his face from him, and as a result David felt desolate? The light of his life had gone away and there was no other comforter. He felt like a fretful child. On the other hand he wrote, 'My soul finds rest in God alone' (Ps. 62:1), and 'I do not concern myself with great matters or things too wonderful for me. But I have stilled and quieted my soul; like a weaned child with its mother' (Ps. 131:1–2).

7

The absent mother

Working mothers

Many mothers are confronted with very hard choices. It may be their natural desire to stay at home and care for their family, but economic constraints make it essential for them to supplement the family income. They have to make as good arrangements as they can for the children under the circumstances and try to see that the children suffer as little as possible.

There are other mothers who are caught in the trap of materialism, and therefore the children end up paying part of the price for the necessary income to keep up the desired standard of living. This seems to be a matter for closer investigation in the light of Christian priorities and human guidelines about the care of and responsibility for children.

Other mothers have had an interesting, stimulating, and perhaps lucrative career which they do not want to exchange for the drudgery of nappy-changing. They do not want to stray far from the promotion ladder, and they enjoy the challenge and responsibility of their profession. They think they will stay at home with the baby for a few weeks and then get back to work as soon as possible, provided they can find adequate help with child-minding. This is a very understandable dilemma: there are the strong pulls of personal status and fulfilment, and also the material advantages as well as the love for the baby. Again, we have to consider the sort of guidelines that we have been outlining, particularly bearing in mind the fact that motherhood is no longer an unavoidable fate, and also the importance to this baby of the 'presence', commitment and love of the focal person in his life. Studies show clearly the importance of the mother and child being together for the first year, at least.

After this first stage has been securely established, most children may be somewhat better able to tolerate their mother's absence during the day, *provided there is a good and consistent alternative mother figure.* It is, of course, necessary for a toddler to begin to separate a little from his mother. In normal circumstances the father is the one who achieves this gradual emotional separation. The difficulty for the child is that while he can relate in concrete terms to his Daddy, protest if need be, or find compensatory comfort, he cannot relate to the abstract concept of 'Mummy's job'; it represents nothing to him except the absence of his mother.

What is a child to do if he is without a consistent mother figure in the background or has an inadequate carer while he tries, with his limited experience, to establish a stable relationship? The outlook for his ability to trust and commit himself at any deep level begins to seem a bit bleak.

Hilary was faced with this sort of decision. She herself had been brought up by her mother and grandmother, because her father had died when she was two. Her mother went to work, but was not well paid, and Hilary remembers the unpleasantness of the financial stringency. Hilary herself became a high-flyer in the City business world, and then she married. Her husband, Paul, had a prolonged illness a short time after their marriage, and Hilary realized that this would be a permanent hazard in their future

75

life. They deliberately bought a house with a mortgage that could be covered by one salary, in spite of their desire for something better. So when their son, Nicholas, was born they had to implement some decisions.

Hilary felt that she had to keep her job as an insurance against the possibility of Paul's future illnesses and consequent unemployment. She stayed at home for seven months before resuming her work, by which time she had secured the services of a nanny who came in daily. She employed this nanny, Agnes, on two weeks' trial at first, while she herself was present to satisfy herself about the quality of care that Nicholas would receive. It was so important that the mother-substitute would be someone to whom Nicholas could relate on a one-to-one basis.

It was hard for Hilary to go back to her job at first. She found her mind wandering homewards involuntarily. Within three weeks of returning to work, her boss asked whether she would represent the firm in America at a business deal. Fortunately, Hilary had foreseen this contingency, and said that she would be glad to go if Agnes and Nicholas could go too. No more was said about it, but she wonders what that did for her promotion prospects.

She gives herself totally to Nicholas for an hour when she comes home in the evening, although she is often very tired. He is still breast-fed twice a day. Hilary had found it hard to establish the breast-feeding routine initially, but says she is so very glad she persevered because of the quality of emotional bonding that was achieved by it. She maintains that it is very important because it is something that she alone can do. She ensures that there is plenty of physical contact with Nicholas when they are together, but she is quite sure that she could not manage two careers if Paul did not share in the housework and the care of Nicholas. At first, Hilary did not know how to react when Paul did some of the mothering of Nicholas. She herself had not had a father whom she could remember and did not really know what fathers were for. Mothers did everything. But she was working hard at understanding fatherhood.

She felt very sad that she was not able to be with Nicholas when he had his 'jabs', which might have frightened him or made him feel sore. It was Agnes who took him to the doctor and comforted him.

Hilary's major problem is that Agnes has to leave, unexpectedly, in two months' time. Hilary is worried about the possibility of a succession of nannies to whom Nicholas will become attached and who will then leave. This is the unpredictable factor in the situation. But at the moment, Nicholas looks like a placid, happy and intelligent little boy who is thriving emotionally. He is obviously accustomed to his father doing things for him and looking after him. Paul was at home for a week after Nicholas was born, but found that going back to work so soon weakened the bond between them. Both Hilary and Paul say that the most important factor in Nicholas' care is the need for reliable and consistent love from committed people. (Mercifully for Nicholas, his parents were not the sort who put a notice in the local paper for a nanny to look after their child, with little understanding of what 'looking after a child' entails, and slight intention of vetting the nanny's experience and ability very carefully.)

Some working mothers, especially if they are lone parents or mothers with a not very co-operative husband, do find it difficult to give adequate time to the child, in terms of both quantity and quality. If there are several children, the problem is even worse. If there are no other adults at hand who can be called upon to help in some way, the children will suffer, inevitably. It is urgent that this sorely pressed mother should do her best to devise ways in which the family can do things jointly, even chores, and have some fun together.

Mothers who leave their children

It is important to try to understand why a few women leave their home and children altogether. Probably most do so with great pain, and only because life has become intolerable. It must also be true that many do not truly comprehend the nature of the vital attachment that a child has to his mother. It is estimated that about 80,000 women live apart from their children in Britain, and an estimated 200,000 children live with their father as the single parent. Only 10–15% of fathers gain custody of their children on divorce.

In her book *Mummy Doesn't Live Here Any More*, Helen Franks records her interviews with women who left their children. She suggests that motherhood is threatened by the current quest for romantic fulfilment and by women's economic dependence within marriage, which may lead to a sense of frustration. Motherhood is also threatened by changed aspirations among women regarding their work or career, by the low status of motherhood and by the high standards of self-sacrifice expected of mothers. Any, and sometimes all, of these factors can contribute towards a situation in which a mother lives apart from her children. Franks writes:

> There is one group of women who come near to confirming prejudices about selfish

and irresponsible mothers. These women are ones who choose to put careers or their personal freedom first in their priorities, though they could provide a comfortable home and support their children.

A pattern emerged among the liberation-seekers and could be identified as

women who married young, perhaps because marriage provided an escape from the pressures of their own family life. Their husbands were traditional, mature – often quite a bit older than themselves – and sometimes devoutly religious. Sex was disappointing, babies were born too soon and life appeared predictable and unrewarding. The marriages were set against the backcloth of the sixties, that decade of new-found entitlement to an enriching sex life, and the seventies with their promises and consciousness-raising messages for women. Then came the eighties and the new materialism. Together with the build-up from earlier decades, the overall effect of modern values has been to make some women want to be free as men are free, to find self-fulfilment, to seek social and career status, to eschew motherhood if need be.

The trend is one that makes motherhood an option rather than a lifelong commitment, rather in the way that modern marriage is an option – if it works, fine; if it does not satisfy, then consider something else. There are women who undertake motherhood in this manner. They claim a right to make a new life for themselves without their children, taking advantage perhaps of a greater willingness among some fathers to keep the family together.[1]

Guidelines when problems arise

When a Christian mother is faced with a domestic situation which seems intolerable, she is under great pressure to follow the pattern of the world around her. It is true that there have been enormous cultural changes in our society over recent decades. But the essential principles that we have been looking at remain unchanged, and are the bedrock against which changing fashions hurl themselves. They provide important guidelines for mothers who have to make decisions in tough situations. They are about commitment, availability, faithfulness and permanence. In order to make it more possible for a mother under pressure to stay with the situation, the extended family, sometimes in the form of the local church, needs to be alert to the difficulties and ready to offer whatever support that mother requires in her care for her family. It is not much good merely to demand commitment without doing something to make it more possible.

Love's authenticity

It comes as a salutory reminder for all of us to consider W. H. Vanstone's comments about love. He says:

> A deprived child who apparently has never known the authenticity of love will yet recognize its falsity. With love it is not as

with food – that those who are hungry will be satisfied with anything. On the contrary, those who are deprived of love are the most demanding and discriminating in what they will receive ... Since authentic love is so potent a support of life, the power to distinguish it from destructive imitations has perhaps evolved as a necessity for survival ... The deprived child cannot describe what he is looking for, although he knows when it is absent.[2]

Vanstone says there are three marks which are recognized as denying the authenticity of love. The first is *limitation*. Limited love often manifests itself in 'kindness'. Kindness under its own name is usually welcome; but it becomes an affront when it masquerades as love. When love dies, kindness often becomes a substitute which, being recognized under the disguise of love, is often thrown back in the face. The second is *control*. Love has become distorted by possession when there is a desire to control the 'loved' one. But the activity of true love is always precarious and vulnerable. The third is *detachment*: the given impression that whatever the 'loved' one does has no power to affect the lover. Adolescents would rather their parents were angry than that they tolerated everything, thereby giving the impression that they do not really love and care.

Mothers' needs

Mothers themselves need to be mothered sometimes. They cannot give out all the time without themselves receiving some personal nourishment. All mothers have times of feeling emotionally unavailable; they may be anxious, exhausted, depressed or even just bored. Once there is more than one child, it is difficult to have the luxury of thinking about only one thing at a time, and it is perhaps almost impossible for mothers to have time for themselves. The nourishment which is so *essential* will come, ideally, from their husbands, but is also welcome from other caring people in their orbit. Without it, a mother cannot adequately mirror back to a child his feelings; she may be too absorbed in concentrating on her own. Then, when the child is miserable and lonely, for reasons he may not understand, he will not be comforted by the warm, accepting presence of his mother. If he is told that there is nothing wrong and he is to pull himself together and stop being such a baby, he will be aware of a brick wall. No-one is interested that he is sad; no-one picks up the messages; no-one tries to help him struggle with the problem. So he has to turn in on his inadequate self for comfort and push his misery under the carpet, thus storing up trouble for another day. Frequent repetitions of this sort of situation lead eventually to his lack of a proper sense of personhood.

Either parent can mirror the child's feelings, but the mother usually has the deeper relationship in the very early months because of her greater availability. But it must be said again that it is not the quantity of time a mother spends with her infant that matters, but the quality. She may have him in her arms, but still not be 'present' to him.

It is not fashionable to admit it any more, but it is nonetheless true that 'the hand that rocks the cradle (or that fails to provide good-enough rocking) rules the world'.

8

The father's place

What is fatherhood?

So, at last, father comes on to the scene. Without him the mother/baby unit would not exist, and all that we've been talking about would be irrelevant. His functioning presence, though different from the mother's, is vital for the health of the child and the family.

There are women, of course, who deny this and want to raise their children without a father. For them, he is only a biological necessity. A recent radio phone-in programme recorded the views of one young woman.

'I am about to become a single mother,' she said. 'I chose to become pregnant and I also chose that the father should have no part in the bringing up of the child. I shall go to work as soon as possible after the birth and earn as much as I can. I shall love the child, try to provide good child care and give it all it needs.'

'Will it need a father?' the interviewer enquired.

'No: I can do all a father can do. In any case, I may marry someone one day in the future. Who knows? It doesn't matter if the man is not the biological father of the child. I have been married before.'

Women who want a baby but not a man are trying to maintain a symbiotic relationship with the baby, hoping thereby to keep their notion of the 'good' and to exclude the 'bad'. Even if the baby is male, it does not matter because he is *her* baby.

It is interesting that there is a significant lack of documentation about the relationship of fathers with their children. Until comparatively recently, the main papers available had to do with such subjects as 'Pregnancy as a precipitant of mental illness in men' or 'Sexually deviant behaviour in expectant fathers' or 'The husband's role in psychiatric illness associated with child-rearing'. The final straw came in a distinguished series of studies on the nature of families in modern Britain. The index reads: 'Fathers – for fathers, see mothers'! This is no doubt due to the fact that most men were out at work for long hours, and leaving the upbringing of the children to the women. As one girl said, 'My Dad was a photo on the mantelpiece. I didn't really know him.' Fathers seemed to be either mad, bad, or absent.

The 'new man'

But all that is changing. The different expectations of women and the economic recession have combined with men's own wishes to be more closely involved in getting to know their children. It is now pleasantly commonplace to see fathers helping with the

housework, taking care of the children more often, out shopping with them, or on expeditions with no mother in sight. Although some fathers may leave home before the children have had their breakfast and may not be seen again until the next morning, most fathers now participate much more actively in their children's lives. The 'new man' is appearing, who is much more of a nurturing father. This new man is trying to discover, explore and express a gentler range of feeling as well as the old, well-tried, tough and assertive image.

But at the same time, says Andrew Samuels, a (Jungian) analytical psychologist, we

> are beginning to meet a new kind of man. He is a loving and attentive father to his children, a sensitive and committed marital partner, concerned with world peace and the state of the environment; he may be a vegetarian. Often he will announce himself as a feminist. He is, in fact, a wholly laudable person. But he is not happy – and bids fair to stay miserable until either the world adjusts to him or he manages truly to integrate his behavioural role changes at a level of psychological depth. Otherwise this man, casualty of a basically positive and fruitful shift in consciousness, will stay a mother's boy. He is a mother's boy because he is doing what he does to please Woman.[1]

This man is competing with his wife to be a better mother than she, and so he both attacks his own fatherliness and undermines her femininity.

The difference between parents

We could ask, 'What is the difference between fathers and mothers?' It is a difficult question to answer except in imprecise language: 'They *do* things differently because they *are* different.' They can, of course, take over each other's stereotyped role very adequately; father can change the nappies and administer the bottle and mother can be the breadwinner. But in *essence*, they are different. Male and female traits cannot accurately be stereotyped as 'masculine' or 'feminine': they are more of an expression of a band of feelings which are simply 'human'. Men and women are discovering a new relationship between themselves and also within themselves: between the masculine and the feminine within the psyche of each person. Stephen Verney suggests that 'many people are saying that the great search of our time is for the discovery of the feminine. My own conviction is that equally urgent is the discovery of the masculine – a true masculinity which can be the partner of the true feminine.'[2]

Stages of fatherly participation

Nowadays, fathers are present at the birth of the baby where possible, and mothers know how much it means to them to make this a shared experience. Fathers know that it makes a difference in the relationship if they are present right at the start. Mother has been having a special relationship with the baby already for nine months, but now father begins to have a relationship with him too, as he looks with incredulity and a sense of awe, and sometimes fear, at this little helpless thing that he has created. He finds, suddenly, that unexpected depths of tenderness are exposed. But many fathers find these powerful, surging feelings difficult to express, and they have nowhere to go to discuss them, unlike their wives.

The early months

The father will be relieving his wife of unnecessary additional pressures and whatever tends to get between her and her baby during these initial months of appropriate maternal preoccupation. He will be providing a facilitating environment for *her*. In this way the mother is saved from having to turn outwards to deal with her surroundings at a time when she is wanting to turn inwards to the centre of her concern – her baby. During the maternal preoccupation phase the father's contact with the baby is usually less immediate and direct than that of the mother, although he may take an active part in some of the care-taking. The mature father is prepared and able to forgo, temporarily, his priority enjoyment of his wife. She concentrates primarily on the relationship with their baby while he concentrates on supporting and encouraging her for the first few months. His job is to create a protective screen around them so that mother and baby can get on with the priority job of establishing the first rudiments of their relationship, which is to have such major significance in later months and years.

Not all fathers find this easy. Many a new father feels threatened by the advent of this new young rival for his wife's love and attention. If the father is not secure within himself and within the love of his wife, he may experience strong feelings of jealousy and rejection, and not be in the least inclined to protect anyone except himself and his own needs for mothering. This may drive him into the need to compete in the mothering of the child, or it may cause him to withdraw into isolation, or to seek other consoling 'loves'. It takes many months for the mother's hormonal system to readjust, and her disinclination for sexual satisfaction with him may reinforce his sense of rejection.

Fathers sometimes have a difficult time in this phase of life, when their own maturity is put to the test and their marriage relationship may be under unexpected pressure. In the close and intimate inter-relationship of family life nothing is straightforward, and the arrival of a new baby often throws hidden cross-currents into sharp relief. Every family member has his or her own internal needs and conflicts, which are sometimes assuaged and sometimes accentuated within the internal dynamics of the family. Some new mothers become so totally pre-occupied with the baby they have produced that they tend to ignore the baby's father, take him for granted in their tiredness, or resent his intrusion into their caring activities.

The father needs to be getting to know the baby, though, naturally, somewhat less intimately than the mother. The extent to which he can do this depends largely on how comfortable *both* parents feel about it. The father has a very special place in his own right if *both* parents can enter into it and enjoy it. Sometimes the mother's feeling of possessiveness can spoil this process; she may want this child all to herself because her baby fulfils some emptiness within her. She might interpret this as being 'responsible' or as being 'protective', but it is not protectiveness, unless the father is actually irresponsible. The mother has to learn to trust her husband, to share their baby, to encourage his caring interest and to relinquish some of her own intense feeling. If she does not, she will be building up trouble for them all in the family dynamics later on by denying the father his proper place.

Attachment to the father

During the twentieth century, the main emphasis by Dr John Bowlby and others has been on the unique and vital attachment bond between the infant and the *mother*. This remains valid and incontrovertible during the first year or so. Recently, much more attention has been paid to the relationship between the infant and the *father*. Milton Kotelchuck (a psychologist at the University of Massachusetts) and others carried out six large and careful studies. They observed that infants cry and become upset when fathers (as well as mothers) leave them, and are delighted and exhibit no 'stranger' anxiety when the fathers return. A four-month-old baby is very aware of the father's presence. The nine-month-old baby's protest (which is its measure of attachment) has been found to be almost the same whether his mother or his father leaves him. Margaret Mead, the anthropologist, has pointed out that forming attachments to both parents has a clear survival value. She also commented that 'from the moment of birth the child grows towards the father'. This concept is not about equal opportunities for the parents but about the nature of fathering.

The child knows his mother but discovers his father. The father, perhaps with little knowledge of early development, is drawing the child towards him and unconsciously working out their relationship together, which is different from that of the child and the mother. While infants become attached to both parents, there are many obvious and subtle differences in style. Play seems to be a more prominent

89

feature in fathers, and care-taking in mothers. The father is more inclined to toss the baby gently in the air, and later play has its rough-and-tumble, physical and competitive aspects; for girls the play has more of an attentive appeal.

It was Advent Sunday. The front of the church was piled up with Christmas parcels to be given to a charity for children in need. The children had brought them up; some big ones with bright Christmas wrapping-paper; some with intriguing shapes and coloured bows, and, in the middle, a beautiful, cuddly teddy bear just looking for someone whom he could love and who would love him. Some of the children were too young to understand what all this was about and had shuffled uncertainly to the front, propelled by an adult, reluctantly offering their special present with an air of great bewilderment. After all that, the children had left for Junior Church and the parents had settled down for the sermon.

One small girl, aged about three, wearing a red dress and with long fair hair tied in bunches, came slinking sullenly back into church, and stood silent and petulant at the end of the pew where her parents were sitting. After a few seconds her Daddy glanced down and without a word took her up on his knee. She snuggled down with her head on his shoulder and scarcely moved until the last hymn, during which she surveyed the congregation from the safety of Daddy's shoulder. Her eyes were clear and her face wore a very different expression from when she came in. Presumably, Daddy understood his little daughter. He could have had a noisy confrontation as he sent or took her back to Junior Church. But he must have sensed what she was needing on that particular morning. Perhaps the love of her heavenly Father was demonstrated wordlessly to her on that occasion, more eloquently than through the splendid Bible story that she did not want to hear. I wondered what kind of fathers the recipients of the Christmas parcels had.

The father has many roles for his children: he is bread-winner, model, Santa Claus and mediator, to mention a few. But the most important part of his fatherhood is his place and interaction as a person within the family – what he *is*.

Separation

As the baby turns into a toddler, it is father who brings a different element into the scenario. It is he who gradually helps both mother and baby to achieve some emotional separation from each other by 'claiming his wife back'. He will be getting in between the mother and the child, offering a more robust type of relationship, with other attractions and experiences. He will also be drawing limits and helping his child to begin to understand that there is now a relationship of three. At first, the child was omnipotent in his own right: the world revolved around him alone. The mother belonged to him: a cosy, exclusive relationship; a twosome which, as well as its times of quiet bliss, had its moments of intense emotion, both pleasurable and infuriating. Now there is a very different situation. The toddler has to learn to share mother with father.

Sharing

Sharing is not easy for someone who is used to being the centre of the stage. Naturally, there may well be some periods of resistance. It is common for children to want to be included in the parental bed at night, as one part of the protest. All sorts of excuses will be invented: 'I'm cold,' 'I'm lonely,' 'I'm frightened,' 'I feel sick.' It is hard for the mother to resist such pleas, as the child well knows. 'What if he really is not well? I would feel awful if . . .' Another form of protest is sometimes seen in the child whose father is away most of the week. The placid, amenable child suddenly turns into an impossible little monster at weekends. At this point the firm and loving father is required to help both his wife and his child to take a step back from each other. His greater objectivity and detachment make it somewhat more possible for him than for his wife.

It is important for the father to intervene and bring balance into the situation, otherwise the mother becomes the 'all-too-present' mother. Problems arise when the father has not done this. Either he has been missing altogether or he has been perceived by the child as having been ineffectual. There are many occasions, of course, when there is a subtle and barely recognized collusion between the mother and child to exclude the father emotionally, even though he is physically present. Eva Seligman writes:

> It is the father who plays a specific and essential role as the mediator of the difficult transition from the womb to the world. Without the father's emotional support, it becomes almost insurmountably difficult for a child to be properly born and confirmed in his own identity and to negotiate the unavoidable separation from the mother, a prerequisite to a satisfactory adult heterosexual commitment. The 'absent father' syndrome encourages a mutually collusive 'embrace' with the mother, nourishing a shared illusion of 'oneness' from which the developing child cannot extricate himself,

leaving him neither in nor out of the womb,
but wedged, so to speak, half-way, half-
alive, half-born.[3]

The absent father, for whatever reason, implies an
absent husband. Sometimes this is the origin of the
'mother's boy'.

Balance

Without separation and learning to share, both
mother and child will become unhealthily stuck in
their dependence on one another. The atmosphere
which allows the child to be totally dependent in the
early months is essential, but dependence is the pre-
cursor to gradual independence. The child who has
never been able to be safely dependent will not be
able to achieve genuine independence.

It is the father's task to begin to introduce some
degree of independence from each other in the
mother and child. This is an immensely important
experience. The child who cannot share relationships, tolerate temporary exclusion, and sometimes
play second fiddle, will find life an uncomfortable
business in all sorts of ways later on. The mother
cannot do all this for her child on her own.

It is also important for the child to see the parents
expressing anger as well as love in their relationship
with each other. Thus, they learn how to fight, to
negotiate and later to be reconciled. A child who
never sees this being contained safely within the
loving parental relationship will often be terrified of
anger in his own relationships and have no idea how
to handle it.

There are similar problems about balance for the
single-parent father, too. Fathers can do a good job of
'mothering', but if the child has experienced the

father as a mother, there can be great confusion for the child when he needs to experience the father as a father.

There are other ways in which parents balance each other. For instance, the father is there to rescue the children from a possessive or domineering mother. The mother is there to intervene on their behalf with an excessively strict and rigid father – unless the parents themselves have each become caught in the web of the other, which they often have.

It is vital for children to sense the secure relationship between their parents, within which they can find their place. Children pick up atmosphere very quickly. The child's inner world becomes very unsafe when there is parental disturbance. Ask any schoolteacher for evidence! The whole process of finding an appropriate place to *be* is made infinitely more confusing for the child if he is being used in some way as a substitute for the love which should be existing between the parents or when one parent is absent and the balance is upset.

The father brings a wider perspective into the child's life, which is the necessary next step after the close relationship with mother has been established safely. The child begins to build a different but very special relationship with him as he gradually introduces the child to the outside world. The father *is*, in fact, the outside world in that he is not part of the initial intimate twosome. He will naturally, therefore, encourage the child to explore and discover all sorts of new things. Both parents will contribute to this, of course, but often the father is the one who brings the excitement and perhaps the physically dangerous element and the aggression which the mother might tend to avoid. In this way, the child is learning vital aspects of limits and protection.

Authority

The father will sometimes be able to absorb some of the frustration which is often directed at the mother, who usually has closer day-to-day dealings with the children. He will also reinforce the law and order which mother tries to establish, and will give her moral support. He will draw, or reinforce, firm boundaries which are so essential for growing children. How many a weary mother, too tired to struggle any longer, has been grateful when father has told the children to get off to bed and stop messing about, in a tone of voice which requires immediate response! This is the proper use of aggression.

In this context, however, we should remind ourselves of Paul's powerful message to fathers: 'Fathers, do not exasperate your children; instead, bring them up in the training and instruction of the Lord' (Eph. 6:4). Children become 'exasperated' by betrayal of trust, and this can take many forms: carelessness, abuse, absence, or ineffectualness, but also undue heavy-handedness.

Many parents share power amicably, and this seems to be the healthiest pattern. Evidence produced repeatedly, over many years, by people working in the field of child psychiatry shows that when a child becomes a problem, this child usually comes from a mother-dominated family.[4] Some women have an internal need of their own to be in control of everything; they automatically inflict this upon their family, and it is sometimes very difficult for them to recognize what they are doing or to stop doing it. Loss of control seems too much like risking chaos. The father needs to be very secure inside himself to take this on and wrestle with it on behalf of himself and the family. Sometimes mothers are thrust, very unwillingly, into the position of domination by fathers who opt out of their responsibility. Both mothers and children often say that they wish father would be more strict.

So it would seem that if power has to rest in one parent more than another, the better arrangement is for it to be with the father. Some may protest that this sounds sexist, but this principle is supported by people who, to their great surprise, have actually discovered personally that it works better. But, of course, father has to be able to wield his authority in a mature and constructive way. Robin Skynner and John Cleese write:

> The sexist implication [in parenthood] more or less disappears if you see the parents operating *as a team* . . . The whole point of a team is that it consists of different people of different abilities playing different roles, but with a common aim. It's no good if everyone wants to be goalscorer or goalkeeper. So the Dad/Mum relationship suddenly looks a bit more like Chairman of the Board and Managing Director. One more concerned with what's happening outside the business, the other more with the inside. And both are equally necessary.[5]

If children do not have a known and recognizable area within which to operate, emotionally and physically, they can become very anxious and insecure. Boundaries are important, too, because they give the child something to kick against. In this way children will discover how far it is possible to go; how to manage their own frustration; how to react to the support that is, all being well, forthcoming in these situations without the whole thing becoming too overwhelming. The child *needs* to be reassured by the fact that even though he does kick, sometimes in fury and frustration, the boundaries do not collapse.

Parenthood is often idealized. What children actually need is *real* parents who can confidently erect any necessary boundaries and deal with the after-effects. It is not that parents should be 'better', but that children should find a place that is secure enough for them to be 'worse' – that is to say, they need to be able to do their fighting, complaining and angry posturing with the sure knowledge that they are loved and safe. Thus children begin to learn that they do not run the world, and to discover their own limits. They will also learn about other people's needs and limits, which they must do in order to understand how the world works and to find their own place in it. By being controlled, a child gradually learns how to control himself.

A good experience of authority lays a foundation for the child to be able to work with other people instead of being someone 'special' whose wishes are paramount. Successful team members do not have a problem with authority, whether they are exercising it or subject to it. The child who has to some extent surmounted this difficult hurdle in early life will find relationships much less problematic later on. This overlaps with the child's experience of being a threesome at home.

It is important for the child's father to be available to perform this function of emotional separation. At this stage, the young child is still trying to piece mother together as a separate person from himself. If he has to see her as the comfortable, soft, loving refuge and also the firm disciplinarian, the child may become very confused. It is much easier if the child can experience two parents who share the load, with father reinforcing and enlarging mother's firmness and drawing the lines. This he can do more easily than mother because he does not have the same extremely close identification with the child. The mother who has the whole burden of providing the strong or strict element as well as the gentleness in the child's life carries a very heavy burden indeed. It is not the quantity of time but the quality of the relationship between the parents themselves and with their children that is important, as they interact with each other.

Fathers contribute in countless ways to the enrichment of their children's lives. One very important contribution which they make is in their children's growing awareness of themselves as girls or boys, and we shall look at this development in the next chapter.

9

Fathers, sons and daughters

The awareness of gender identity develops slowly in the infant, and comes about partly due to inherent factors and partly through cultural conditioning. By the age of four, children usually divide automatically into groups of their own sex. In addition to the growing interest in where babies come from, little boys become very affectionate and possessive of their mothers, and little girls of their fathers. They often exhibit marked signs of jealousy towards the parent of their own sex. This accounts for the attempts to interfere when parents are alone together or show each other affection (hence the need to come into the parents' bed at night). These feelings are intense because of the important nature of the internal struggle that is going on, and because children do experience their feelings extremely acutely. Therefore, they should be taken with all seriousness, though they will not pose a real threat when the parents are secure in their relationship with each other.

The child learns his or her sexual identity by modelling himself or herself on the parent of the same sex and at the same time observing and experiencing the parent of the opposite sex. This is made all the easier when each parent is comfortable and aware in his or her own sexuality. The child will see that both parents have many similarities but that they each also enjoy being vitally different. If there is some blurring of the images, the inevitable result for the child is some confusion and uncertainty in his or her own sexual identity. For instance, a boy may have a weak, non-participating or absent father who offers no identification model; he may have a compensatory forceful mother who has terrified him. Thus he often has later difficulties in his own sexual orientation. Similarly, if a girl does not have a particularly loving mother who is comfortable with her own sexuality and with whom the girl may identify, she may find herself in difficulties with her own sexuality later; especially so if she also had to contend with a father who is more interested in her physically than is appropriate. The premature arousal of sexual awareness by the father unbalances this girl's emotional development. If she is subjected to actual sexual abuse by him, or any other male, the results will, of course, be catastrophic.

The father's presence and the part he plays in the life of his son, and in a different way in the life of his daughter, are vital to their developing a comfortable sexual identity. His positive attitude toward the 'feminine' side of his own nature as well as to his masculinity, and the pleasure he takes in the femininity of his wife, will be affirming to the sexuality of his growing children. They, in their turn, will have the same positive attitude to themselves. The same principles apply for the mother, of course.

Increasingly, the boy identifies with his hero-figure and companionable father. He observes and learns the things that men do, and he likes to be included in their activities rather than having to stay at home with the 'wet' girls. He develops a preponderance of the well-known 'masculine' attributes of body and mind within himself: strength, incisiveness, reason and practicality. If there is a problem, he finds ways of solving it and has a 'man-to-man' discussion with

Dad; he does not sit around pondering what it feels like. The boy also gradually begins to discover some of his 'feminine' attributes of sensitivity and gentleness and how to exercise them in relation to himself and other people. Sometimes that can be a struggle.

Fathers and daughters

The 'lover stage'

It is well known that there is often a very special relationship between a father and his daughter. Even the way he holds his newly born daughter is different from the way he holds his son. The girl wants to adore him, flirt with him and enjoy being admired and spoilt by him, as well as learning how men function. There is the potential in every girl to fantasize about being the most important woman in his life. A woman's sexuality is influenced powerfully by her relationship with her father, and it is a style that they have with each other that goes on over many years. If the father enjoys her pretty dress, her first efforts at make-up and jewellery, her smile and her beauty, she will gain confidence in herself and her sexuality. Conversely, if he is threatened by 'feminine wiles', he might frown and thus encourage her to be more reserved and bury her ability to engage in courtship play. There are many gradations of response, but the level at which the style is set largely depends on the warmth of the father's response. It is easier for a daughter to leave her father geographically than emotionally. In his book *Fathers and Daughters*, William Appleton observes that

> the more a woman understands her *father*'s effect and makes use of this knowledge, the more she will be able to enjoy her *husband* sexually, emotionally and intellectually, the freer she will be to pursue and advance in her career, the better she will be as a mother of her own children and the richer her life will become.[1]

The father is the first man to whom she gave her heart; and how he reacts affects strongly her future with other men.

It is the mother's turn to be secure in herself and in her husband's love at this stage, as it was his turn in the first year, so that the father–daughter relationship

102

is not interfered with by the mother's jealousy and rivalry. But these things are often easier said than done!

The changing scene

This dynamic interplay in the lives of two developing and changing people cannot remain static. A father may be good with his daughter at certain ages and in specific ways. He may be delighted when his three-year-old imitates her mother but may show no interest when she is fully grown. He may enjoy helping her with her homework but may never enquire about her friends at school. Because no man is perfectly able to adapt to all the phases of his daughter's developing sexuality, almost every woman grows up impaired to some extent by her father's faults and mistaken reactions. But that need not be irrevocable!

When his daughter is struggling through her adolescence, the father is usually struggling through his forties, and for both of them it is a hard time. They are both asking, in different ways, 'Who am I?' and 'What is life all about?' Neither wants to lose the cosy closeness, but she is no longer the adoring little girl because they are both changing and she sees him differently. She is older, so she can acknowledge some of the real weakness that he, like all other humans, possesses. It is hard for him to lose her adoration and to face reality, and it is hard for her to have to move away from her childish security with him as they both leave the fiction of the 'lover' phase.

This separation is sometimes accompanied by anger and disappointment. She wants autonomy but still needs his support; she perceives his help as inter-ference, advice as orders and concern as babying. He must find a way to help her even though it is resented, and to offer advice that she probably will not follow. Fathers who are preoccupied with their own mid-life problems are usually short of patience with all this and have little spare energy to negotiate delicately with their touchy teenage daughters. As a result, there may be stormy battles, or else they may just withdraw and become unavailable.

Unless a girl can see the failures in her father, she will remain a child in her relationships with other men, expecting them to be heroes, endlessly patient and supportive – in other words, a father to a little girl. This spells trouble for the future! If the father can accept her anger and criticism arising from her disappointment in him, two good things may happen. She will gradually be able to detach herself from emotional dependence on her father; she will then be free to invest some of her interest in other men and have more realistic expectations in her relationships with them. As she does this, she will return to her father as an adult, and they may then be able to enjoy each other on an entirely different level. But it takes years for a father to adjust to the emotionally adult status of his daughter and for him to be able to accept that she is also sexually adult.

The whole business of the emotional interrelationship of a father with his daughter is very complex and has a profound effect on her subsequent relationships with men. The influence of mothers on their sons is also important in similar ways. Boys will learn how to relate to women and how to appreciate their own sexuality and that of the opposite sex. They will often be seen to be 'practising' courtship on their mothers, and it is important for her to co-operate appropriately in a way which will enable him to feel safe and 'try his wings'.

A father–daughter relationship is not simply a

replica of a mother–son relationship, with the sexes reversed. Nor is the identification between mother and daughter psychologically of the same order as the identification between the father and daughter. Observation will show that all this is a very complex area.

Disillusionment

As the young child's sense of his own omnipotence diminishes, he is comforted by the knowledge that at least his parents are omnipotent. Gradually, however, the older child will begin to take on board the fact that father and mother have faults and limitations. This is very hard to accept, and the young child usually resists this realization because of its implications of insecurity. But for older children it is another step towards independence, and children may begin to regard their parents as 'boring' or 'old-fashioned', and begin to look in other directions for their attachments.

The child himself is not God. His parents are not God: they have only been God's representatives. Now this person, growing into adulthood, has to discover the real God for himself or herself, not merely absorbing without question what the parents have said. How is this person, in youth and age, to interpret the apparent limitations of the omnipotent God? Sooner or later it will be his or her turn to relate to life's painful circumstances, which make people ask, 'If God is loving, why did he allow . . .?' and 'If God is omnipotent, why does he not do something about . . .?' and 'Can God be both loving and omnipotent?' There is, of course, no known answer to these questions, but the child who has had not a perfect but a good-enough, loving father and a good-enough, loving mother, or good-enough consistent parent substitutes, will be in a much better position to live with the tension and the unknown. This person will have experienced trust, faithfulness and commitment, without which life becomes intolerably flimsy and faith irrelevant.

God the Father

We cannot end a discussion of fathers without reference to the prototype for all fatherhood. Of all the metaphorical descriptions of God in the Bible (including his motherly nature), that of a father occurs most often. Scripture describes God the Father's loving care, his watchful attention, his willingness to let us be dependent and independent, his discipline and his constancy. We learn what a good father is by studying the fatherly nature of God.

variety of difficulties. Behaviour problems increase at home, worries and anxieties are more prevalent, self-esteem may be affected, performance at school declines, and behaviour problems are often reported by teachers.

An eight-year-old boy, Stuart, and his six-year-old sister Miranda, attend the same school. Stuart is very quiet and amenable, but Miranda's behaviour is very disturbed and disruptive most of the time. The head-teacher requested an interview with the parents and discovered that they had been divorced for two years. The mother and the two children had had to move from the large and comfortable house in a salubrious area to a small house in a different neighbourhood. Residential change occurs for many families after divorce, often involving a drop in the standard of their accommodation and the neighbourhood in which they live. These changes lead to changes in schools and friends, thus adding to the emotional burden a child has to bear.

'I know Miranda is a terrible problem,' said her mother. 'She has been ever since we split up. But Stuart is fine. He never gives me any trouble.' The discussion continued and the headteacher mentioned a few things about both of the children which had been a concern to the staff. Eventually the astonished mother said, 'Well, Stuart has never mentioned any-thing about the divorce. He seemed to have taken it so well. I didn't think it had affected him.'

It is easy to understand that one troublesome child was enough, and this mother was glad to think that at least one of them was 'taking it well'. Stuart had no need to speak openly about it, because Miranda was making the protest on behalf of both of them. His mother did not know that he lay in bed at night wondering what would happen if she left too. What if she died? Who would look after them? What would they do? These terrible silent fears were too great to speak about because there was no known answer to them. Stuart just went about with this huge black cloud hanging over his young head.

The cost for the family

Virtually all children are extremely upset on learning that their parents have decided to divorce, even those who have been keenly aware of marital turmoil. Parents, too, are upset at separation, even if they instigate it, and also feel a range of intense emotions: anger, loneliness, grief and dependency. The crisis period usually lasts about two years and is brought about by many factors: the separation into two households; the children's loss of their father on a daily basis; the father's loss of home life; for some, continued conflict with the ex-spouse over money or custody; the significant decline in the mother's standard of living; her sole responsibility for the upbringing of the children, and pressures to take on employment or expand her hours of work. Predictable daily routines give way to chaotic lifestyles, less attention to homework, late bedtimes, and tardiness or absence from school.

The cost for the lone parent

The lone parent tends to be unable adequately to support and nurture the children, and is more likely to be irritable, to over-react to any misbehaviour, and to fail to set appropriate disciplinary limits. This pattern is especially the case with mother–son relationships and is seen as an important factor in boys' conduct problems. It is a time of conflict, anxiety and uncertainty.[2]

On a radio programme a woman who had been divorced for fifteen years was describing her experiences. He ex-husband had problems in maintaining two households. 'Being poor takes a lot of time, trailing round the shops looking for bargains,' said the woman. 'If anyone knew what bringing up children by yourself involves they would think twice before embarking on it.'

One lone father was emphasizing what hard work it was to bring up children on his own. His wife had died, so he had given up his job to care for their two daughters and two sons. He now does a part-time window-cleaning job from nine till three in order to be there when the children come home from school. They are all right financially, he says, 'but it's terribly hard work on your own. I have no social life and I hardly ever have adult company. There's more to life than money for a parent.'

One mother in such a situation cannot send her three-year-old boy out to play anywhere because she lives at the top of a high-rise block of flats and she cannot afford child care. They are under each other's feet all day long driving each other mad, and she burst out angrily, 'I'm wasting my life looking after the health of this child.'

It is extremely hard for some single parents to cope with the unassisted burden of looking after the children, the financial struggle and often poor housing conditions. Parents and children experience psychological and social problems, decline in family functioning and other changes in daily living. Their difficulties are apparent.

The cost for society

A broken home is now such a familiar experience, however, that it has become part of society's accepted norms, and people appear to detach themselves from its deep and lasting impact as from the atrocities which we see so regularly on television. They are horrendous, but familiarity breeds a sort of indifference. Almost every child at school knows other children in the class whose parents no longer live together and who are the victims of a broken home. Every child to whom I spoke seemed to feel, nevertheless, that he or she was different when it happened to him or her; and children cannot bear to be different.

I have a five-year-old friend who was telling me in shocked tones the other day about a boy at his school. This boy, Darren, has just been suspended for the fourth time. He spits at anyone, throws bricks about, picks up scissors and cuts the other children's hair, snips off all their sunflower seedlings, and puts his hands in paint and then wipes them on the teacher's pullover. Once, he stamped on the teacher's glasses in the playground and then pulled his tie as tightly as he could. Needless to say, he is the despair of the teachers and frequently prevents the other children from learning or playing.

I enquired what was wrong with this child. Is he mentally ill? No. Neither is he educationally subnormal. He does require individual tuition, but the special schools are being closed so that all children can be in the community, and the local authority is axing one-to-one teachers because of the expense.

Can you imagine the inner emotional turmoil of this child who is at war inside himself? He does what he does because he is in such confusion and anger, and without a place of safety within himself. It comes as no surprise to learn that his parents had divorced, but not before Darren had been subjected to scenes of violence and abuse. His situation now is less violent physically, but still emotionally volatile. Darren may be an extreme example, but he is by no means an exception.

Angela was twelve when her parents began to separate. Her father had been working away from home for a year or two and then started coming home less and less regularly at weekends. She was fifteen when her mother told her, in a studied effort to be casual, 'By the way, I've been to court about your Dad.'

'Why has she been to court?' thought Angela, and began to ask a few questions. Her Mum told her that it was necessary to get the finances sorted out because Dad was not giving her a proper allowance for Angela, and she could not afford to keep Angela herself.

'So what do you have to do to get a proper allowance?'

'Well, I told you. I went to court.'

'What do you mean, you went to court? Are you getting a divorce, or something?'

'Yes. It was made final today,' Mum admitted at last. Angela was stunned and silent. Until then, she had been quite unaware that her parents were about to make their separation so final. Divorce is like a dreaded illness. It happens to other people, but not to me.

'Oh ... thanks, Mum ...,' was all that Angela could find to say. She felt helpless and furious.

'And that's how I heard that my parents were divorced. I was shocked. But then I realized that it's all happening all round. Everyone does it. It's all part of life. Nothing abnormal. So I stopped thinking about it. That was five years ago.

'Soon after the divorce another guy moved in with Mum. I always hated him. He's dead lazy; he just sits in front of the telly all day, smoking. I try not to be in the house much when he's there. I spend as much

113

time as I can in other people houses, or in the park, or if it's wet, in the library. I got a bit of a bad name at school because I went with the boys. Mum wants to get rid of him now, but she can't.'

It is a well-known fact that one of the side-effects of a broken home on adolescent girls is that they are more likely to engage in early and more promiscuous sexual intercourse. Are they trying to prove to themselves that they are still wanted by someone and that there might still be some 'love' around somewhere?

It is said that 119,000 British teenage girls become pregnant every year, of whom one third (or more) have abortions. Probably some young women have deliberately got themselves pregnant in order to be able to get away from home and get council accommodation and state allowances. They would say, 'What else is there to do if you are thrown out of your home or have to leave it because life there is intolerable?' This, no doubt, has something to do with the fact that one of the fastest-growing social problems in Britain is the 'single-parent family' phenomenon. It is causing great political concern, as well as being a tremendous drain on the taxpayer.

In all the heated public debate, however, it is interesting that most of the emphasis focuses on the matter of finance – the cost to the country or the poverty of the single-parent family. Little is heard about the *emotional* effects on the girls themselves, or on the unidentified boys, or on the children who are being brought up under circumstances of possible homelessness and poverty, without a father. The fact that the girls are repeating their own history seems, largely, to escape attention.

Angela was one of the fortunate ones. The church community, of which she had been a peripheral member, spotted her and looked after her. Now she does not want a close relationship with any boy (or, at least, not for a very long time) because of her experiences.

Drugs

Mike sat slumped over his mug in the mobile soup kitchen. He may have been about seventeen. His clothes were rough and his face had the blank expression of someone who has no hope. He had been coming to the soup kitchen on and off for several weeks but rarely spoke to anyone. One day, after several tentative approaches, one of the volunteers tried cautiously to engage him in general chat. He answered in monosyllables. Eventually he said he used to live at home but his parents had split up after much rowing. His Mum took in 'a new guy who didn't like me. We had lots of rows and eventually Mum threw me out.' Mike has no job: he was a packer for a short time but was laid off. He has no home; he made one or two attempts to see his Mum, but he felt unwelcome, so he now dosses around – miserable, lonely and a prey to whatever comes along. He is already experimenting with drugs. There is a lot of money to be made by exploiting the misery of some of these youngsters. This misery begins in the home, not in South America or the Customs and Excise Office.

The National Child Development Survey was launched in the 1950s and followed the progress of 17,000 children all born in one week in March 1958. It found that children who had experienced parental divorce or family breakdown were roughtly twice as likely to have failed to obtain any qualifications by the age of twenty-three as those whose families remained together, whatever their social class. More left school at the minimum age with no 'O' levels (there was no

GCSE then) or 'A' levels, and were not in full-time work. Those who were in work had mainly unskilled or manual jobs.[3]

Homelessness

Until recent years in Britain, it was unheard of to see people sitting by the roadside displaying their cardboard placards: 'Homeless and hungry'. Not any more. It is commonplace, especially in the big cities. Where do they come from? Are they genuine? Are all their homes so terrible? Is Mike one of them? Homelessness is another of the fastest-growing social problems of our day, which, as we are reminded constantly, arouses much political and social concern.

Crime and violence

There is an alarming escalation in juvenile crime, car stealing, burglary and even murder, but the rise is particularly noticeable in children as young as four and five. In some of the children this is associated with truancy and drug and alcohol abuse. There may be various subsidiary reasons for all this personal and social distress, but the ills usually have their roots in an inadequate or broken family background – no close family ties, no parental supervision, and often acute shortage of money.

It all makes very depressing reading, but the list could go on, with teenage suicides, eating disorders, depression and more. I have just been involved with the funeral of Nigel, a young man of twenty-two. He had been out to the pub for a drink with his girlfriend, with whom he wanted a very intense relationship. She was much more laid back about the whole thing and included some of her friends in the evening, much to his chagrin. He went home afterwards, apparently quite normally, and hanged himself in his bedroom.

Why? Whatever makes a young man want to do a thing like that? The photographs of him as a young boy displayed such promise; his smiling, eager face seemed to be waiting for life. Enquiry revealed that he was six when his father suddenly walked out; he has never been seen since by any of his family. After that, Nigel became quiet and seemed to withdraw inside himself and preferred to be alone. He did not like talking to people and had few friends. His mother was relieved when he found this girlfriend, but Nigel wanted to possess her emotionally so that she would not suddenly slip out of his grasp as his father had. He was desperate when he could not do this, and the time bomb exploded.

The role of the non-custodial father

The role of the father is central to the adjustment of children after divorce. Short-term studies show that the high involvement of an emotionally healthy father after the marriage breakdown has a significant bearing on healthy child development. There is inevitable damage of some sort to a child if he or she loses contact with one or both parents. Both parents have permanent responsibility for any children they create, even if these parents cannot live together amicably. That responsibility goes further than the financial obligations; it is about the child's sense of *belonging*. One child, whose father was now cohabiting with another woman and her children, was heard to ask his teacher: 'Is my Daddy *my* Daddy any more?'

Fathers often lose contact with their children within two years of the break-up. It is sometimes difficult for them to find neutral ground on which to meet the child, and the infrequent encounters acquire a sense of artificiality which gradually becomes intolerable for the father and the child. If the child is very young and without much verbal skill, the relationship can be difficult to maintain on this infrequent basis. Fathers often feel sad and frustrated about this, but do not have the stamina to pursue the issue with all its complications. If the child is older, and the father does not have a convenient place in which to entertain the child, or does not want to, it is all too easy for him to degenerate into a Santa Claus figure who is just there to give the child some new treat. If he is not in a position to offer these treats, he may disappear from the scene through sheer embarrassment.

There are some Access Centres around the country in which the non-custodial parent may meet the child in protected surroundings on a 'drop-in' basis. They are manned by volunteers and are often in a church hall, or some similar place, and are approved by probation officers and social workers. In most of the centres, 90% of the parents are fathers. The contact between some fathers and children seems, however, to have little meaningful content.

One child's behaviour was so unruly that his father had the utmost difficulty in communicating with him at all. Another toddler was so small that all the father could do was to trail along after her rather pointlessly. One father was playing cards with his daughter and buying crisps and Coke at frequent intervals, but communication between them on a personal level seemed to be very stilted. It did not seem that there could be any long-term future in this sort of meeting.

Another father was certainly making contact. He was desperate for total custody and was waging an all-out battle to get it. He was making maximum physical contact with six-year-old Samantha and one-year-old Adam, and they obviously knew him well. He bought many presents for them because that was the best way he knew of demonstrating to them that he very much wanted them to live with him on a permanent basis. He was feeling very frustrated about the situation, having thought, without much perception, that he and his wife were 'an ideal couple', though they 'did not communicate about "inner things"'. After each of these sessions, Samantha and Adam were returned to an angry and resentful mother. They were caught in the cross-fire of the parental battle.

Problems also arise when a child grows up resenting one or both parents for the divorce and for the circumstances which brought it about. Eleven-year-old Mandy said, 'If I ever meet my Dad in the street I shall kill him. I hate him for what he did to me and my Mum, coming in drunk every night and beating us.' Obviously, when there is much unresolved feeling, there will be long-term after-effects.

Home is a crucial factor in personal security. One mother complained that her daughter's bedroom gives the permanent impression that the burglars have just left. Her son uses the house as a 'pit stop' before another race around the track. But they all know that this home is where they belong, where they are accepted, loved and safe. There is a high degree of trust.

11

Family patterns

Reconstituted families

After the breakdown of one marriage, the individuals have probably learnt something about themselves and about relationships. They may have greater maturity to bring to the second marriage. And yet research shows that second marriages are no more stable than first marriages and that the rate of divorce for second marriages is increasing. Half of the fathers who divorce lose contact with their children within two to three years. Disconnected from their families, many people, especially men, enter into another marriage fairly quickly. Often, problems which were not resolved satisfactorily the first time will surface again the second time, unless a policy of 'peace at any price' pushes them under the carpet.

The children

Again, in second marriages it is often the children who are the main casualties. In a radio introduction to the book *Parenting Threads*,[1] Stephanie Calman compared stepchildren to refugees, with their confused feelings as they go to and fro at weekends across borders between one household and another. There are different customs about bedtimes, different rules about mealtimes, and different attitudes to many things. At holiday times the children's friends are not there to play with, or their skateboard or bike is not available. These little things can become big irritants. Ms Calman urged the importance of keeping the children in contact with all the changes and involving them in discussion as things go along.

But, good as that is, it is second best when a child's home is no longer a place of refuge, or his bedroom has to be shared with children he did not invite. It ignores the point that research suggests that children would rather have their own parents stay together, even if there is trouble from time to time, than the upset of separation or divorce. The parents may not love each other any more, but the children usually have a special bond with one or both of them; and, if the parents part company, the children are then left with the double pain of losing the parent as well as the family home. Those who favour divorce for the sake of the children are on shaky ground.

Seven-year-old Martin used to hear his parents arguing downstairs when he was in bed. The name 'Malcolm' was often mentioned in anger. Martin was afraid because his friend at school had parents who were divorced and he did not want to be in the same situation. Martin went through agonies because he knew that if his parents did split up he would have to be separated from one or other of them, and he could not bear the thought.

His parents did separate; his father did move out eventually; and, soon after, someone called Malcolm came to live with his mother. Martin was told how nice Malcolm was and that he was going to be his new Daddy. But Martin did not know what to think about Malcolm or how to relate to him. After all, he had been the person about whom his real Daddy had been so angry, and it seemed that Malcolm had pushed Daddy out. How could he love him or be nice to him? He just wanted his own Daddy back and for everything to be safe like it was before. He could only explain to people that 'Malcolm isn't my real Dad.' Moreover, there were now two of Malcolm's children in Martin's home. He did not know them nor did he want to. Many a night he cried himself to sleep, secretly and alone, wondering why his Daddy had left him and somehow feeling betrayed by the Mummy he loved. He felt helpless and confused.

Julia, aged twelve, was quite matter-of-fact about her situation. At her boarding-school she used to say openly, 'I'm only here because my parents don't want me. Before the holidays there's always an argument between them about who is going to have me. I get in the way of Mummy's career, and Daddy has a girlfriend, so I'm in the way there, too.' Julia was described as 'very sweet, helpful, generous and co-operative'. Superficially it would appear that the home situation had had no effect on her. But what would her chance with either parent have been if she had not been 'sweet'? What might have been going on below the surface?

The emotional effect of combining two families can add complexity, anxiety and confusion to an already complicated situation. Boys who live in such families are more likely to have left home by the age of eighteen than those who live with lone mothers or with natural parents. They enter partnerships at a young age and are more likely to have become fathers by their early twenties, without the maturity and stability to sustain such relationships, thereby perpetuating the cycle of emotional deprivation. Girls who were not living with both natural parents at age sixteen were significantly more likely to have left home at a young age than their contemporaries who lived in intact families. They were also more likely to have a child by the age of twenty and to have had an extra-marital birth. This was the same whatever the social class, the ability score or the school-leaving age.[2]

Statistics show that both mother and father have a one-in-three chance of having been married before and of bringing stepchildren into the second marriage: 2.5 million children live in reconstituted families. Until fairly recently the prevailing wisdom was that changes in family composition had few, and relatively small, persistent effects on the lives of children. With the advent of more long-term studies in which children were followed into their adult years, however, evidence is beginning to suggest strongly that the effects of marital disruption may carry through into adult life.

Is the child's age significant?

The research literature does not provide a definite answer to the question whether the age at which a child experiences the breakdown of his parents' marriage has any short-term or long-term effects. Virtually no official research has been done on the effects of divorce on infants, and there is considerable disagreement on the effects of divorce on adolescents. Some researchers think that adolescents are less vulnerable to such a striking change in family life because they have their own peer networks and relationships with adults outside the family. Others think that adolescents who are already somewhat detached from their families and involved with problematic peers will be even more harmed by divorce.

There are comparatively few long-term studies on divorce, since it has only fairly recently become an accepted part of modern society, but the evidence from the USA (where divorce rates have been high over a longer period than in Britain) would seem to suggest that we should not be too optimistic about the possibility that divorce might ever become less damaging.

A gradual process

Parental disharmony and family dysfunction have usually existed for a long period before the divorce. The parents have 'fallen out of love' and have gradually become estranged from each other emotionally and sexually. So they may be beginning to turn elsewhere for consolation – to work, sport, other individuals, or even, inappropriately, to their own children. By contrast, positive marriages, where the parents have a warm and close relationship and honest communication, promote healthy development in their children. Evidence has shown that there are observable differences in the behaviour of the children of such families as compared with the children of marriages which do break up. Behaviour disturbances seen in boys after divorce had existed years before the parents separated (and a similar but less pronounced pattern was found for girls).

A brave new world?

We may ask whether our new freedoms have made the world a better place. Where are we going? What, we may wonder, did Lewis Carroll have in mind in *Alice in Wonderland* when he recorded the following conversation?

> 'Cheshire Puss,' Alice began, 'would you tell me, please, which way I ought to walk from here?'
> 'That depends a good deal on where you want to get to,' said the Cat.

'I don't much care where . . .' said Alice.

'Then it doesn't matter which way you walk,' said the Cat.

'. . . so long as I get *somewhere*,' Alice added as an explanation.

'Oh, you're sure to do that,' said the Cat, 'if only you walk long enough.'

Alice felt that this could not be denied, so she tried another question. 'What sort of people live about here?'

'In *that* direction,' the Cat said, waving its right paw round, 'lives a Hatter: and in *that* direction,' waving the other paw, 'lives the March Hare. Visit either you like: they're both mad.'

'But I don't want to go among mad people,' Alice remarked.

'Oh, you can't help that,' said the Cat: 'we're all mad here. I'm mad. You're mad.'

'How do you know I'm mad?' said Alice.

'You must be,' said the Cat, 'or you wouldn't have come here.'

If you prefer, there is the more prosaic verdict of the Authorized Version: 'In those days there was no king in Israel: every man did that which was right in his own eyes' (Jdg. 21:25).

Or you could accept Dorothy L. Sayers' definition of sin as 'producing out of our own wits the standard by which we should live'.

What can we do?

The results and ramifications of broken family relationships create the fastest-growing and greatest social problems in the West today. Children have to endure the anguish of emotional fragmentation as 'normal', and, frequently, as we have seen, they have to bury the accompanying feelings because there seems to be nothing else to do with them. Women's magazines and radio programmes are full of discussions about ways of coping with the various stresses. Children's television programmes frequently include items designed to help the young viewers who are struggling with the lack of a father, or with two fathers, or with the suspicion and rivalry created by the second mother's or second father's children who have come to live in the now overcrowded house which was once home.

For sure, there have been unhappy marriages since time began, but divorce or the absence of one parent has become a widespread phenomenon at the end of the twentieth century. There are constant reports of political concern, recommendations and suggestions about how 'the values of family life' can be re-established. But what sort of family life are we talking about? The sort we have at the moment does not seem to present an optimistic future. Values have changed; ideas of family must change. The question we have to ask ourselves is: 'What shall they change into?'

The nuclear family?

Does all this suggest that we should strive to re-establish and strengthen the nuclear family with its two parents – father the bread-winner and mother looking after the home and children? Is the nuclear family the ideal? Clearly, there are thousands of well-adjusted, happy families whose children grow into healthy, balanced adults. But since we are aware of the high level of distress, we have to ask whether nuclear families are under greater pressure now than they used to be. Much of the litany of upset, disappointment, rejection, anger and fear is caused by the poverty of personal relationships within families. This small, close-knit nuclear unit is an institution which was almost bound to explode under the pressure of the modern world.

In former times, families used to stay within their family group, geographically and relationally; thus there were plenty of members of the extended family to help carry the family load and share in the business of child care. Expectations were minimal, families were large, and survival was the main preoccupation for the majority. For others, who lived in affluence, there was usually a loved and faithful nanny, the mother substitute, who often stayed with the family into her old age. But there was often, for the boys, the ghastly separation to boarding-school at some incredibly early age.

Nowadays, greater mobility brings freedom and certain other advantages, but it also brings a greater degree of isolation. Thus, the family has now become much more of a private affair. With its diminishing size and lack of easy access to supportive kith and kin, each individual within the family is much more exposed to the dynamic emotional forces which push and pull both from within and from without. Parents are expected to meet each other's emotional, social, sexual, physical and intellectual needs, completely and exclusively, with little outside support. That seems to be bordering on the impossible. Children are enmeshed, inevitably, in the emotional cross-currents.

Which alternative?

All family cohesion is achieved at some cost to the individual. Some say that for them this cost is too high, so they have renegotiated the contract and brought in new forms of family life. Thus we have a variety of family units: widespread cohabiting, because people are not prepared, for whatever reason, to make a public undertaking of commitment as a new social unit, preferring to privatize their arrangements; 'reconstituted families' with children within one family belonging to different parents; parents who do not live together but still maintain their parenting from a distance; children who only have one functioning parent; married people who choose not to have children; women who wish to bring up children without a male partner but in a supporting female network; and we still have the struggling nuclear family. All this is 'normal' in the contemporary world.

Recently, at a sixth-form college in the north of England, students were discussing attitudes to sex, with a small panel which included a fairly senior member of the Department for Education. He wore a suit, collar and tie, spoke articulately, and looked old enough to be the grandfather of most of the young people with whom he and the other panelists were engaged in debate. Inevitably, the subject got round to Aids. The main burden from the floor (in spite of all the heavy publicity there has been) was: 'We don't know enough about it;' 'We don't really know how you catch it;' 'It's all due to unemployment;' 'You go out to the pub, get drunk, and before you know what has happened, you've had sex, and if it's the first time, you're all right;' 'The Government should do more about it;' 'We know it happens, but it won't happen to us.'

The Education gentleman was given the last word in the programme. 'Two parents are every child's birthright. No-one here has said anything about families, parents, or grandparents . . .'

The rest of his sentence was lost in an outburst of derisive laughter from the floor.

The problems created in the community and for individuals by this confusion are in the forefront of the thinking of Government policy-makers who introduce new White Papers at frequent intervals. We are warned that the breakdown in society which we see on every side is due to the breakdown in family life. Right-wing politicians advocate the strengthening of traditional family ties and values; left-wingers want more freedom and financial provisions to enable split families to have a more secure base. In the words of Ann Kelleher, presenter of a BBC *Public Eye* programme, 'Is personal fulfilment incompatible with family ties? While we are contemplating this, we are watching the richest of human institutions going straight down the drain.'

A biblical concept

We have to recognize and accept that a multiplicity of family forms characterizes life in most parts of the world in the latter half of the twentieth century. One form of family structure is common to us, but we have to beware of regarding it as the sacred norm. The nuclear family – that is to say, husband, wife and one or more children – is not a biblical concept but a product of the modern Western world. This insular view of the nuclear family marginalizes people who do not belong to it and creates loneliness.

The Old Testament is characterized by the importance of family and tribal cohesion, which led to personal identity and corporate commitment and responsibility. The family lies at the heart of God's creative purposes. Husband and wife were to live together in some kind of family structure with known boundaries and clear roles, and to create other members of the species to be in their image; the family also included married children and their families, and slaves and their families.

A Rocha is a Christian field study centre in Portugal which Peter and Miranda Harris have been running for ten years. They have had a constant stream of resident visitors and have been trying to implement the principles of extended family life. In his book *Under the Bright Wings*[3] Peter says:

> One secret of success was evident . . . and that was the necessity for a clearly defined central family unit which was then able to keep the boundaries open to outsiders. If the central unit lost its distinctive identity, both adults and children became uncertain. In the case of the children, they needed to know to whom they were answerable. In the case of the adults, tensions and difficulties rapidly overran idealism if some sort of authority structure was not maintained. Where a clear family identity was established with a husband and wife who took responsibility for all that went on in the house, then life was in general harmonious and creative for everyone else.

Germaine Greer is not known for her conservative views, but even she says that the extended family is not a dormitory of double beds.

Internally, the task of the family was to hand on

from one generation to the next the knowledge of the nature of God, the known experience of his historic faithfulness to his people, and the health-giving laws and traditions. The family's internal relationships were to mirror the overriding relationship of love and permanent commitment between God and Israel (Ex. 4:22). Externally, it was to be a tremendous contrast to other religions, which represented either an impersonal god in natural elements, or God as One as distinct from God *in relationship*. Thus, the family was to be the primary vehicle by which God and his will were made known to the people. In the New Testament the concept is re-stated in Jesus' declaration: 'For whoever does the will of my Father in heaven is my brother and sister and mother' (Mt. 12:48). David Brown and David Atkinson comment:

> Family is not merely a social arrangement, a conventional institution for the sake of exercising certain functions. Family is 'a way of being' in this world: a way of being which is essentially communal and personal because that is the way God is. The central focus of the Bible's view of family is not on

131

the institution but on the quality of personal relationships within it.[4]

Those relationships are characterized by the loving responsibility of husband and wife for each other, for their children and for other members of the family; trustful dependence by the children on their parents; and space for each to grow within the knowledge and experience of love and trust.

In her book *Family Matters*, Sue Walrond-Skinner draws a helpful parallel between the human biological family and the spiritual family to which Jesus was referring.

> The task of the human family is to enable the individuals within it to mature beyond the self by learning to relate to others, and by struggling with and living the paradox between autonomy and interdependence. This means intimacy (without fusion) and differentiation (without separation). The family members will then be in a position to leave the family home and engage in the business of living in the world. Members of the spiritual family will have similar experiences of individual nourishment and maturing so that they will be able to leave the Father's house and engage in the struggles of the Kingdom.[5]

The challenge

This presents us with some food for thought about the nature of our own family and the relationships within it. There is no guarantee that a family home will be 'good enough' merely on the grounds that it is said to be Christian. The task of parents is still to portray by their own dependability an image of what God is like; to let the child actually see and hear them praying in dependent trust about everyday things (Johnny's visit to the dentist or Mary's exam) and the wider world issues; to engage with the children when they ask why God seems to do such extraordinary things at times, and why he sometimes does not do what we ask, although he has told us to believe that he will.

The start of a new family and its relationships is usually marked by a man and a woman 'falling in love'. We shall look at this in the next chapter.

12

Ready for marriage?

The state of marriage, they say, is like a besieged city. Half the world is trying to get in and the other half is trying to get out. Let's look, first, at the people who are trying to get in, and who may then want to get out.

The chemistry

Teenagers Matthew and Rachel and their mother were having one of those spontaneous discussions about life that arise round the kitchen table. 'So how did you and Dad end up together?' was the question, with unspoken implications for their own future choices.

Mum could not be precise, so she said, 'I don't really know. It must have been the chemistry.'

'What chemistry? What is the nature of this chemistry?' they could have asked. Most people wonder why we fall in love with one specific person rather than another, when there is often a fairly wide choice.

On one level the response to this is that 'attachment behaviour' comes into play. One specific person arouses in us feelings of belonging, safety, being understood without having to explain anything, and other powerful, basic responses. That specific person produces these reactions while other people do not. When the first real love affair ends, there is usually great anguish and heartbreak because of the painful significance of broken attachment.

But what decides which specific person will be the object of our 'love'? What constitutes this chemistry? There are conscious, recognizable, physical attractions – blue eyes, red hair, tall, dark and handsome, and so on. There are possibly certain admired attributes – musical, intelligent, athletic, even rakish, and so on.

The unconscious part of being in love

There is a mixture of conscious and unconscious factors which come into play. Everyone can pinpoint these obvious attractions. But there is something more – that 'something' which cannot be defined; that 'something' which can bind two people together so strongly that they are prepared to fly in the face of their own common sense, and sometimes the warnings of other people; that 'something' which cannot let go, even when the relationship is over in real terms.

These strange and apparently irrational attachments are usually directed towards someone who reflects a part of ourselves, sometimes a hidden or unacknowledged part of our own personality. It is the fact that this person is 'carrying' something of mine that accounts for the *strength* of the attachment. There is something about that person which 'fits' me. I feel complete, blissful and 'in love'! I am, in fact, searching for my own psychological wholeness through another person, 'my other half'. Part of me is reflected in that person, in addition to any personal attributes that he or she may have. Therefore, I am tied closely in a 'fit' in that relationship, the precise nature of which I am not consciously aware of. When we speak of the 'in love' state we are usually including strong sexual passion and an intensity of emotion that is not experienced in other affectionate relationships.

One of George Bernard Shaw's favourite pastimes was to make quips about marriage. He said that when two people are under the influence of the most violent, the most insane, most delusive and most transient of passions, they are required to swear that they will remain in that excited, abnormal and exhausting condition continuously until death do them part! (He was, of course, referring to being in love and to the wedding ceremony, which is not the same as marriage.) Freud expressed being in love more pithily as 'a temporary psychosis'; in other words, losing touch with reality!

Loving

The difference between being 'in love' and 'loving' is crucial. In the 'in love' state I am, to some extent, seeing a reflection of myself which conditions my expectations and reactions. I am also inferring that I will love you while you continue to fulfil these expectations. (But what am I supposed to do when

136

you cease to do that?) Shakespeare's lover in *As You Like It* is 'sighing like a furnace, with a woeful ballad made to his mistress' eyebrow'.[1] 'In love' sees what it wants to see in the loved one and is often at variance with the view of less biased onlookers. On the other hand, 'love' is not so blind: it can see very clearly that the loved one has feet of clay and sometimes rather smelly socks, but it continues to love, even though the initial expectations have largely ceased to operate.

The struggle of marriage is about growing from the 'in love' stage to the 'loving' stage: being able to tolerate and love Prince Charming with his weaknesses as well as his strengths; being able to kiss Beauty even when some of her beastliness becomes all too apparent. Not easy! There is inevitable disappointment and disillusionment in the continuous intimacy of marriage, as well as the surprises of joy and delight. The struggles which engage happily married couples and those whose experiences may cause them to part are essentially the same. It is the attitude with which the partners address the struggle that will influence the outcome.

False expectations

Romantic love

False expectations can mitigate against growth in the relationship. One such expectation is the idea about romantic love in which all needs will be met within the marriage; there will be an ideal 'togetherness', fusion, and no separateness. This has strong overtones of the imagined idyllic state of babyhood, with a mother who understands everything without having to be told and who never has any other business to attend to except the care of her beautiful baby.

The idealizations and distorted perceptions are

heightened by maintaining a certain distance from down-to-earth reality and expecting the delicious 'in love' syndrome to continue. It is one thing to be having exciting evenings at the theatre or leisurely country walks, or even doing temporary jobs together. It is another to see a bleary-eyed man who can only grunt at breakfast time, or to come home at the end of a tiring day to an untidy and harassed woman who is also tired through struggling with domesticity all day. Romantic love has its intoxicating place and is often the point at which a relationship starts. But it is *not* a sturdy enough plank on which to build a marriage!

Sally was a student when she met Anthony, who was ten years older than she. He was good-looking, had a well-paid job, and seemed to pursue her with exciting determination. She had just finished her finals when they married. Before the marriage, Sally had had some serious doubts about whether this was really the right thing; but she had a rosy dream about what marriage was like: '. . . and they all lived happily ever after'. Sometimes Anthony seemed to be rather depressed; but Sally assured herself that it would be all right when he had her love around all the time. Also, she had begun to feel pressured into making a decision because 'he was that much older, and it did not seem fair to keep him waiting'. But he was fun to be with and she looked forward to being married and having a family. Her own parents had a very happy marriage and she expected hers to be the same.

But on the honeymoon the first severe disappointment struck. Her husband seemed more interested in preparing for what was, to him, a very important presentation which he had to make soon after their return home. Thereafter, his work always took priority. Also, he declared quite definitely that he did not intend to have children: the world was too awful a place to bring children into. (He was referring to the outer world, but he was speaking from the point of view of his own inner world.) Sally was amazed by all this. They had not discussed it before marriage; the possibility of childlessness had not occurred to her.

Four years later, she was acutely distressed because she realized that she was trapped into a seemingly impossible situation. Sex was virtually non-existent; hugs had to be asked for; money, though plentiful, always had to be accounted for, and life seemed totally without joy and hope. So utterly different from what she had expected initially in her romantic love! In an attempt to build something of a life for herself, she had found a job at which she was doing well. But now the problem was that she had met someone who seemed to promise some of the things which she was missing so sorely. Almost inevitable! Why had no-one warned her before all this started? Would she have listened if they had? What happened to the marriage preparation?

Sally had taken her marriage vows very seriously, and so this pretty, intelligent, warm-hearted and ingenuous girl intended to stick it out. What was she to do now? She tried to convince herself with increasing desperation that God had told her that it would be all right to marry Anthony and therefore he would give her the strength. In her own desire to achieve her rosy dream she had not been able to recognize that God's voice might have been speaking in her own initial doubts: the 'voice of God' became all mixed up with her own. Perhaps the voice of God was getting mixed up with her own again now.

One of the reasons Sally gave for not leaving Anthony was that 'he would fall to pieces if I did'.

She really believed this, but could not see that somewhere lurking about in her unconscious self was a
strong bond that kept *her* in this unpromising situation, with all its destructive implications. She labelled
it 'taking her vows seriously' and 'believing that God
would help her'. She found it very hard to face the
possibility that she was staying with him because of
her *own* fear of falling apart if she had to stand on her
own feet, which she had never had to do before. The
question for Sally to consider, actually, was not,
'Shall I escape from this situation?' but 'Is there something in my emotional economy which needs a
deeper look? Could there be something in me which
fits in with something in Anthony to produce this
negative situation?' Sally may very well require some
skilled, outside help to look at some of her own needs
and expectations. If Sally were just to leave Anthony,
without working on the situation, she might well find
herself in a similar position later on with somebody
else.

There are, of course, times when people do behave
selfishly, and stubbornly deny their need to change
and to recognize the hidden parts of themselves.
Sometimes the result is so destructive that parting
company seems to be the only constructive alternative and the lesser of two evils. It is not the marriage
promises in themselves that are crucial. It is the person who makes these promises, with all the inner
luggage he or she is bringing to the situation.

The need to be happy

People who use the yardstick of romantic love to
gauge the health of their marriage are particularly
susceptible to being seduced out of their real marriage by an exciting affair which promises elsewhere
the romantic love for which they are still searching.

A mother in her mid-thirties was considering splitting up from her husband. 'We don't do anything for each other any more. I'm not satisfied. Every woman has the right to be satisfied, and I want to recapture it before I am too old,' she told the headteacher at her son's school. The teacher was appalled that what seemed like a frivolous reason for ending a marriage should be allowed to cause such anguish to a child. She herself knew the cost of staying in a marriage 'for better, for worse'. She also had burning in her ears the anguished comments of the children who have divorced parents. She had just been trying to comfort one small girl whose 'friend' had told her, with the ruthless cruelty of a child, '*Your* Daddy doesn't love you!' Another boy had come to tell her that his (divorced) 'Daddy is going to have a baby. I hope it won't be a boy, because he won't want me any more if it is.'

In her understandable anger, the headteacher complained about 'this adult woman who was fretting because at the age of thirty she was not experiencing the buzz that she received when she was nineteen. The trouble with this woman is that she married when she was not emotionally ready.' She had been 'desperately in love', but had not known the difference between being in love and loving; nor did she seem to have grasped it now. She had had her children while she was still too young, and now she felt she had never lived and was being cheated of something.

'The common theme that runs through much of the children's misery,' the headteacher continued, 'has at its heart the parents' complaint that "I am not happy. I need self-fulfilment." The consequences of this philosophy are dire' – not just because of the immediate effects, which are terrible vulnerability, utter disconsolateness, and meaningless confusion, but

141

because of the dreadful feelings of guilt which most of the children have as a result. In some way which they cannot understand, this must all be their fault. As well, there are the long-distance results influencing their choice of partner in later life and their attitudes to marriage.

There is also a ripple effect. In answer to the question, 'What is your greatest fear?' one little girl wrote in her school-book: 'My greatest fear is that my Mummy and Daddy will get divorced.' Her parents had no wish to get divorced, and as far as anyone knew there was no reason for her to fear it, except that she had seen for herself the distress and grief of another child in her class.

An escape route

Another false expectation is that marriage will be *the answer to life's problems*. This notion is specially attractive to the young and the lonely. Adolescent marriages carry with them an inbuilt risk of failure, because by its very nature, adolescence is a time of change and experiment and not a time for making long-term, binding commitments. In Britain the divorce rate for women married in their teens is twice as high as that for those married between twenty and twenty-four and three times as high as that for those married between twenty-five and twenty-nine. The adolescent may be desperate to leave the restrictions of family life, and may see marriage as an escape route. Alternatively, marriage can be a halfway house, as they leave the security of one nest for the security of another. Only later, when they feel trapped again, or constricted by the confines of the new nest, have they developed sufficiently to want to launch out into life. Then it may mean leaving the partner who has come, by then, to represent the restrictive parent.

The fear of loneliness

The idea of marriage is also attractive to the lonely single person who is no longer an adolescent. It is so easy to forget the wise saying that 'Most people marry because they are lonely, and most people get divorced for the same reason.' Many people may see the wedding as a point of arrival rather than as a point of departure into marriage. Often we do not recognize our expectations until they are disappointed. There can be some great periods of deep loneliness within marriage, when the struggles of reality and disillusionment are being engaged with and the relationship is growing. Bringing up very young children can also be a very lonely business. It may be that for women, more than for men, marriage and motherhood seem attractive answers to the disturbing questions, 'Who am I?', 'Where do I belong?' and 'What is the purpose of life?'

The search for wholeness and healing

The search for psychological wholeness has close connections with the early years of life and the way feelings were expressed or suppressed, handled or avoided in childhood experience. It is based on how I learnt to see myself and other people; how I reacted to intimacy, separation, sharing, trust, dependence, sexuality; to all those foundational stages of reciprocal relationships; to the unmet needs of which there are remnants in everyone. The ability to sustain, or the failure to sustain, a covenant relationship which binds individuals together has its personal and psychological roots which stretch back into childhood.

Not since infant days have I been addressed so lovingly, touched so intimately, and, in some ways, so totally dependent. Now, in this second relationship, some of those sexual feelings, conflicts, needs, anxieties, fears of rejection and distortions will surface again, unbidden. In the new context of committed love, care and attentiveness, some of those feelings which have been buried may become integrated into the personality for the first time rather than being split off into their dark and dangerous hole where they carry on their sniping operations without being recognized. This loving acceptance of me and my fears, and a gradually deepening trust, can have a profoundly healing effect, as it does in many marriages.

But unresolved emotional problems can overwhelm the couple. If two people who are very deprived emotionally bring into their relationship demands, needs and heavy expectations (of rejection or gratification), they will soon exhaust each other and be consumed with frustration and anger. Their love was really the love of a small baby who wants its own needs met, totally and immediately. Current emotional difficulties bear the indelible marks of childhood experiences.

Having considered some reasons for exercising caution before plunging into marriage, we shall turn in the next chapter to the dynamics of attraction and successful marriage.

13

A marriage that works

Factors affecting the choice of a partner

Similarity

Some people are attracted to each other because of their similarity in background, interests, lifestyle and inner personality structure. Their attitudes to life are the same and therefore they find an easy reflection of themselves within each other, whereas difference and otherness feel threatening. Together they feel safe and can project all the darker sides of themselves on to the outside world. At an extreme, some Christians (as well as other people) do this, reinforcing themselves in their opinions and attitudes, and refusing to acknowledge challenges that would arouse fear and an uncomfortable rearrangement of their inner attitudes. These challenges are said to come from 'the world' (and some of them do in reality); but, because they pose a threat, they are dismissed as 'worldly' and not relevant to their entrenched position. Thus, the couple can continue their life in comfortable security from the pains of growth and change. But such a marriage can become stifling because inevitable differences cannot emerge and be tolerated.

When we try to preserve a relationship by a fearful or possessive clinging to the other, no real love or life in the relationship is possible. It becomes a suffocating embrace. The paradox of real love is that it is not expressed in how close we can get to each other. It is expressed in learning what is the right amount of space between each other. The Lebanese sage Kahlil Gibran expresses this in *The Prophet*, when asked to speak on marriage:

> Love one another, but make not a bond of
>   love:
> Let it rather be a moving sea between the
>   shores of your souls.
> Fill each other's cup but drink not from one
>   cup.
> Give one another bread but eat not from the
>   same loaf.
> Sing and dance together and be joyful but let
>   each one of you be alone,
> Even as the strings of the lute are alone
>   though they quiver with the same music.
> Give your hearts, but not into each other's
>   keeping.
> For only the hand of life can contain your
>   hearts.
> And stand together yet not too near
>   together:
> For the pillars of the temple stand apart,
> And the oak tree and the cypress grow not
>   in each other's shadow.
> You were born together and together you
>   shall be for evermore.
> You shall stay together when the white
>   wings of death scatter your days,
> But let there be spaces in your
>   togetherness.[1]

But this is very difficult for people who, because of their experiences in childhood, interpret separation and distance as rejection. The couple whose bond is based entirely on similarity will have little to communicate about. Their objectives will be to reinforce each other's defences against the 'outside world', and any resolution of their own potential differences will not be part of their agenda because they will not be recognized.

People of similar personality structure who are not so rigidly defended can tolerate to a greater degree the confrontation to their conservative attitudes without losing their bearings. Their marriage can mature; they can grow personally and also have very productive relationships.

Complementarity

Trudy had been delighted when Neil proposed to her. She had always been very aware that she had no particular claim to fame. She had been born illegitimately and her adoptive Christian parents had chosen and idolized her as their only child. They had prayed for her regularly. They were 'ordinary' people, not very perceptive, who loved Trudy in the way they knew best. They had rejoiced in her good looks and ability, but her performance at school had not been outstanding, and she regarded herself as rather less than mediocre on every level. She was warm-hearted and affectionate, but she had some difficulty in expressing this side of herself to her parents because they seemed to expect so much of her. In due course, Trudy had become one of the helpers in the church Youth Fellowship.

There had been a great fluttering in the dovecote when Neil arrived. He had seemed to inject life into the whole group and had set things humming. In no time he had become the accepted overall leader. He had also seemed to inject life into Trudy, and she had begun to find a creative and expressive part of herself which had been dormant till then.

Neil had come from a family where achievement was the priority requirement and love was undemonstrative. When Neil had encountered Trudy he had found a warmth which he could not express for himself. She had provided the 'facilitating environment' in which undiscovered gentle and caring parts of himself could begin to emerge. They both became enriched as individuals as their relationship deepened.

Mutual defence

In the inner dynamic of the marriage relationship there are many ways in which people use each other as a defence against their own feelings. A very angry husband can obviate the necessity for his wife to look at her own anger if he will carry it for her. This anger can be a defence for both of them against recognizing the underlying painful depression which they share. A wife may see herself as the longsuffering, patient and good wife (and perhaps privately see herself as the better Christian!). Her husband may experience her as 'a Victorian schoolmistress' and fail to see that she embodies for him all his own self-critical, self-destructive, guilty, self-directed accusations. He can safely blame her because of his own inner need to be disapproved of. It may be immensely difficult for both of them to see and achieve any change in the situation. If such a release should come, and either partner shifts his or her position on the marriage 'seesaw', the other's must of necessity change.

In Ibsen's *The Doll's House*, we have the story of Nora. Her husband assumed that she knew nothing about what went on in the outside world in which he struggled, and he treated her in the way her father had, as a pampered little plaything not to be taken seriously. For a while Nora enjoyed this, but life's events made her grow up, and eventually the time came when she was not prepared to tolerate being petted any more. After a great row with her bemused husband, she declared that she had been a doll to her father and a doll to her husband, and she was now a woman in her own right. With that, she stormed out, leaving her husband emotionally paralysed. Nora had changed the position of her weight on the seesaw. The story leaves us there, but it would be comforting to suppose that, in time, both Nora and her husband were flexible enough to negotiate a middle position with which they could live.

We all need defences to protect us from emotional pain. Emotional ill-health arises when the defences are too high and rigid to tolerate any flexibility or to admit of any change. Anything – for example, rejection or a domineering attitude – which symbolizes the early lack of care can strengthen these defences, but fortunately the new experience of a 'good-enough' spouse can reduce and modify these defences, leading to a richer experience of life.

Stalemate

Sometimes people become locked in acrimonious and blaming exchanges and cannot work out their relationship. The underlying quarrel in marriage is frequently about how often each can be the baby. Continuous blame is often a message of despair. It is born of very early childhood experiences in which there has not been much basic trust in the powerful adults, who seemed either not to care or not to want to be helpful. Deep, hidden feelings of being vulnerable and deprived are aroused.

People and relationships remain static when their 'inner child' has become stuck at the demanding stage of 'You must meet my needs,' or 'You must carry my inner luggage for me, because I find it too painful to own and carry it myself.' Such people frequently find intimacy and attachment frightening at the deepest level. They want closeness, but cannot cope with the intimacy that closeness involves. They also cannot cope with the inevitable separation and aloneness which is the other side of the coin of intimacy. They want closeness all the time. All that is needed must be available, and anything short of it is useless. These conflicting fears often mean that their way of asking ensures that they do not get the closeness they say they want.

As two people come together they bring with them two separate life histories, but they are more likely to explain a floundering marriage in terms of current stress than in relation to the past life experiences which have produced these two people. Most of us fail to recognize this when we run into trouble as adults. The cerebral learning we have accumulated as children is only a small part of what we are: a larger and immeasurably influential part is what we have absorbed into our emotional bloodstream. A safe, reliable, good-enough mother 'out there' has, all being well, become assimilated within us. Now that she is 'in here' too, we can go on from that safe place to engage in the risky business of making other relationships. Secure attachments in childhood provide inner resources later on to cope with the demands of commitment in marriage and other relationships. If no such safe place or safe attachment exists the position becomes much more complicated, as many divorces demonstrate. The cycle then moves into the next generation.

Safeguards

Time together

One obvious reason for the growth in the marriage difficulties which some couples encounter is that they do not make enough *time* for one another in order to keep more or less in touch with each other's emotional needs and rhythms. If there are not enough opportunities to relax together, to play and to laugh, and sometimes to talk at length, removed from the pressures of everyday life, there is every possibility that a marriage relationship will become sterile and superficial. People do not stay at the stage at which they were on the wedding day; change can overtake us without our recognizing it if we do not pay attention. But when talking at length involves the painful business of revealing inner wounds and fears, and the person's life expectation is of rejection, there is often little incentive to make this time. There are always less risky things to do.

Communication

One important way of keeping in step with each other is adequate communication about things other than the routine affairs of daily life. There are times when it is necessary for one partner just to listen to the other, trying to understand the significance of what is being said, without interrupting or attempting to explain or justify. This involves a disciplined and voluntary silence while the other person is speaking, and then checking that what has been meant is what has been heard. Then it will be the turn of the other person to present the situation as he or she experiences it, also checking that what has been meant is what has been heard. Many a fracas has arisen over an unnecessary misunderstanding. This sort of communication involves time and freedom from outside interruption, but it is abundantly worthwhile because of the dividends in growth and trust which can develop.

An obvious reason for growing distance between a couple is inability to communicate. How do I communicate when what I have to say may be hard and very painful, or will make me look foolish? I shall not feel like exposing this vulnerability if there is insufficient trust that you have enough willingness and inner resources to hear, receive and respect this pain. It is not an easy road, and to take the risk of accepting and being accepted requires real commitment. But this is the way to growth. There may be some false starts, but it will become easier with practice.

Some children have been fortunate enough to experience parents who have respected their vulnerability and who have shown that powerful feelings can be contained and managed. Such people have a much better adult ground from which to communicate and negotiate about adult needs, fears and differences.

How does one communicate when one's life experience has inculcated the stiff upper lip and the value of repressing one's needs and feelings in order to keep the show on the road?

Murray's marriage had fallen apart without his even noticing. He was a hard-working and successful solicitor and his whole life went into his work, although when he was at home he was kind and a very good father in all ways. He had a privileged background, but was one of those people who could not relate to others on a personal level; it had to be through work or golf. Meanwhile his wife was the chauffeur, babysitter, cook, housemaid and general factotum until she was not prepared to put up with it any longer. When the parting of the ways came, Murray was devastated, but had no idea how to approach his own personal problem. It was apparent that he was distressed, but he also seemed to be paralysed. He epitomized the dual problem of being unable to communicate and being unable to tolerate intimacy, although he said he wanted it. The children's main preoccupation is the hope that their parents will come together again; but they do not understand that it is not as simple as that. Their son cried initially but now will not speak about it. He went to school the day after he had been told that his parents were separating, and felt different from all the other boys. The grandparents were heartbroken; they were desperate to help, but felt powerless.

Sex

People who are afraid of verbal penetration in social intercourse are often afraid of sexual penetration. People who must have everything under control in daily life are often afraid of too much excitement, abandonment and risk in bed. Intercourse, social and sexual, epitomizes intense intimacy and closeness but also inevitable ending and separation, if only temporarily. There can be such a feeling of horror about the aloneness and emptiness that follows intercourse that there can be a distaste for physical intimacy and oneness.

The enjoyment of bodily intimacy often reflects early emotional development. If, as a baby, the person was handled with enjoyment, and the lovely little naked body was admired, and if there were no subsequent damaging experiences, that person usually seems able to enjoy sexual intimacy naturally. But people who did not experience pleasurable physical contact with their parents may find themselves unable to enjoy their own body or that of another. If they have always been held awkwardly, had little play with and sharing of their mother's body, and had no interest shown in their own body and what it could produce, they may, in their turn, be stiff and ashamed of nudity. Sexual delight, or lack of it, is the direct heir of infancy. C. Clulow and J. Mattinson write: 'Problems of sexual intercourse are as interactive at an unconscious level as some of a couple's intercourse out of bed ... Some couples assiduously hang on to a sexual problem as a defence against facing up to a much wider problem in their marriage.'[2]

Commitment

Marriage is a public but personal contract underwritten by law, but a piece of paper does not constitute a marriage. There is also the emotional contract which, because of its unconscious nature, often has a very binding quality when one partner regards the other as the source of his or her emotional wholeness. The legal contract is a very useful container in which a couple can work out the complicated business of creating the new life of their marriage while retaining their own individual lives.

The progressive task of marriage is to convert the initially unconscious choice of a partner into conscious commitment: within marriage being in love can grow into loving. 'This requires some ability to acknowledge and manage one's own infantile feelings rather than inflexibly project them into the partner,'[3] write Clulow and Mattinson. If the partners are committed to their own growth as individuals and to the growth of the marriage, a healthy situation can develop within which growth can be based on trust and a redundant past can be abandoned. But this is not done without sustained effort. There are times of great turbulence and anxiety while this is being worked out. At those times it is useful to have the external container in the form of the legal contract. It is not the institution of marriage but the commitment that is usually at fault.

God's will: 'It feels right'

Most of us will have heard young people saying about their intended marriage, 'It will be all right because we're Christians.' Not so! Not so! We can never put the responsibility on to God for making our marriage successful. There is no guarantee that any marriage will ever be a 'success' – though marriage is such an individual business that what is a success for one couple would be a disaster for another. God's will is much more than a lovely feeling of 'rightness' which can tend to obliterate all other indicators. 'Rightness' often has more to do with our current psychological needs than anything else. In marriage we embark on a massive and not always easy journey of discovery, and the only guarantee we have is that as Christians we have the resources of the Holy Spirit within us to face the unknown. And the Spirit of Christ will have been demonstrated originally in our experience of the Christ-like acts and attitudes of our parents (the facilitating environment) until the time when we become spiritually aware.

This does not mean of course, that God has no interest in our choices. On the contrary! But it does mean that we need to be as aware as possible of what we are doing; not floating along on some grand idea. It also means that the community has some responsibility for enabling us to make an intelligent and sensitive choice; to make a choice which, as well as having the initial feeling of completeness, involves discerning whether there is enough foundational stability to make this a viable marriage worth working on. If 'in love' can go hand in hand with 'loving', there is good reason to suppose that God's will has been at work. (But one often cannot be sure about God's will until after the event, so, in order to ease the tension of uncertainty, we tend to look for signs!) The test of a good relationship is not 'in the beginning of a thing, but in the continuance of the same until it be thoroughly finished, which yieldeth true glory' (as Sir Francis Drake said when he was taking on the Spanish Armada!).

The ebb and flow

Marriages have their rhythms and tides. A low tide does not necessarily indicate a mistaken choice. High tides are exciting, but low tides reveal all sorts of unexpected things. The question is not 'Did we make a mistake?' but 'How do we engage with these new and unexpected elements in the situation or find a way of living with them?' In his book *Marriage Diffi-culties*, Paul Tournier says, 'You have problems? That's quite normal: all couples do. As a matter of fact it is a good thing. Those who make a success of marriage are those who tackle their problems together and overcome them.'[4] It is important not to throw out the baby of a developing marriage with the bathwater of its growing pains.

David Runcorn encapsulates some of the problems about communication and the struggle to grow in his book *Touch Wood*:

> Within the joyful experience of falling in love there can also be an awakening of deep fearfulness. Our inner world is being invaded. We are losing our privacy. This is not in our control. For something as great and central as human love to enter our lives a space must be created somewhere. So someone described the feeling of 'whole areas inside being demolished'. The experi-ence of love is also an experience of dying for it requires our complete self-giving. Equally, the building and strengthening of a relationship requires a willingness to admit to the loveless, fearful and untrusting parts within. No love will survive by clinging only to the good bits.[5]

14

The trauma of divorce

Tolstoy begins his great novel *Anna Karenina* with the words:

> All happy families are alike but an unhappy
> family is unhappy after its own fashion.
> Everything had gone wrong in the
> Oblonsky household. The wife had found
> out about her husband's relationship with
> their former French governess and had
> announced that she could not go on living
> in the same house with him. This state of
> affairs had already continued for three days
> and was having a distressing effect on the
> couple themselves, on all the members of
> the family, and on the domestics. They all
> felt that there was no sense in living
> together under the same roof and that any
> group of people who chanced to meet at a
> wayside inn would have more in common
> than they, the members of the Oblonsky
> family, and their servants. The wife did not
> leave her own rooms and the husband
> stayed away from home all day. The chil-
> dren strayed all over the house, not know-
> ing what to do with themselves. The
> English governess had quarrelled with the
> housekeeper and had written a note asking
> a friend to find her a new place. The head-
> cook had gone out right at dinner-time the

day before. The under-cook and the coach-man had given notice.[1]

The entire Oblonsky household had become disjointed because of the dislocation in the pivotal relationship between Oblonsky and his wife.

Divorce between a particular couple never happens suddenly. It will have been coming for a long time before it actually arrives, although it may be that one of the partners has not been aware of what is happening. It is sometimes possible to forecast a divorce even before the marriage has taken place, because of the misalignment of the partners or the improbability of one or both of them being mature enough to grow within the marriage. The majority of divorce processes begin during the first five years of the marriage, when disillusionment is at its height and reality begins to take the place of idealization, or when 'being in love' fails to mature into a settled 'loving'.

The legal contract

Although there had been huge files of correspondence with lawyers, it still came as an unbelievable chill for Ian when he read the letter in the brown envelope that dropped on his doormat. It confirmed, in a bald statement, that the marriage between him and Mary at St Margaret's Church in their home town in June 1984 was now dissolved. All the brilliance of that day and everything that had gone into the years between then and now – just dissolved by a court of law! The financial arrangements were almost settled, custody and access were agreed and all the respective responsibilities were sorted out, on paper. The ends were tied up. The person he had thought he knew so well and whom he now saw and had to relate to, was no longer his wife and partner. On paper the marriage was over.

But the court could not dissolve the fact that a large slice of their lives had been lived together, that there had been a great deal of fun in the beginning, and that there were now three other people, their children, to carry on the effects of their marriage.

The emotional aspect

People sometimes say that divorce is now so commonplace that we ought to be 'better at it'. What does that mean? Presumably it means that it should be possible to arrange a divorce tidily and in a 'civilized manner', with everyone knowing what is happening, and everyone's best interests being taken into consideration, thus causing as little pain as possible in all directions. The intention of the Children Act in 1989 was 'to make the situation less traumatic, for children and for parents'.

One highly intelligent mother said, in a debate, that in her view her child receives a much better quality of parenting now that she and her ex-husband are divorced. They can come together with more enjoyment and undivided attention to the boy than when they all lived together. She actually meant that there was much less overt pain for the parents in this arrangement. Her son had been conditioned not to give vent to his real question: 'Why doesn't Daddy come home with us?' He knew the answer very well in his own intelligent brain, but that did not prevent his heart from wanting to ask the question. Most children would prefer to have both parents living with them continuously and to risk the ups and downs of family life, unless there is an intolerable degree of violence, physically or emotionally.

Divorce is like the amputation of a limb. Occasionally we see horrific representations of the way in which surgical amputations were performed 300 years or so ago, with the patient being held down forcibly by a group of tough-guys while the local surgeon-barber detached the offending limb. No sterile dressings and no anaesthetics were available then. Now, of course, we are 'better at it'. Amputations are carried out by skilled surgeons under 'ideal' conditions with everything to ensure sterility, the minimum of pain, a healthy recovery and a speedy rehabilitation. Does that make an amputation desirable? It may be the extreme resort to the lesser of two evils, but even under 'ideal conditions' life can never be the same again for the patient. Amputation is undertaken only to preserve life or to relieve intolerable pain. The patient will always carry the scars, and life will inevitably be affected by this major 'surgical insult'. Obviously, procedures should be as civilized as possible, but the result is still an amputation, with all the intense emotional and physical trauma involved. The difference between divorce and amputation is that it is not only the patient who carries the scars. Children of the divorce also carry the emotional scars of this involuntary amputation for the rest of their lives.

As experienced by children

The effects depend on the sex, age and personality of the child, the quality of the parenting with the remaining parent, the degree and quality of contact with the parent who is leaving and whether there is a remarriage. Most children suffer immediate distress when a parent leaves home, and this may last for a few years, but the long-term impact may not be

161

known for decades. However, the ranks of neurotics, alcoholics, delinquents, and people with personality disorders, sexual problems, violent behaviour and psychiatric disorders have an above-average incidence of divorce in their family background, as we have seen.

Charlie's mother had come down to see him one weekend at his school, and had taken him out to tea to make the announcement. He was totally shocked by this unexpected news. The boy in the bed next to his was lost for words and, that night, as they were about to go to sleep, could only manage, 'Sorry about your parents. Goodnight.' Nothing more was said for the rest of his school life, as far as anyone knows. Long after he had left school, Charlie met a lively young woman whom he wanted to marry, but she was reluctant to respond because 'I never know what you are feeling: you will never tell me.' With considerable and painful persistence, she made him face the feeling part of himself that he had buried long before.

In adolescence

A housemaster at a well-known school was considering the effect of divorce on the boys who had been in his care. He could not think of one boy who had not been affected in some way – some more, some less – and he agreed that the way in which children are told about the divorce is of immense importance. During the emotional disturbances of puberty, a boy needs a very secure background in which to come to terms with himself. If the home situation is shattered, it makes life increasingly complicated. Often school is the safe place, continued the housemaster, because home is so fraught, or the boy does not know which address to call home, or is not sure where he will be during the holidays. Sometimes the acrimony in financial terms becomes very distressing for the helpless teenager who is caught in between it all while the court settlements are being arranged. It may be that he has been assured that everything will be all right: Dad will continue to live in his London home and the boy will live in the country with his mother. But before long, the country home is being sold, money seems to be less available, and circumstances begin to change, thus reinforcing the general sense of insecurity.

Of course, children try to resolve their inner conflicts and soothe the pain of their 'amputation' in one way or another. They may find it hard to relate to other people at any depth and can burst out from time to time in scenes of irrational violence, especially if this is the way they have seen their parents reacting to problems. Many, like Charlie, withdraw into themselves and become very quiet. It is not usual for boys (as it would be for girls) to engage in lengthy discussions about their parents' affairs – they usually just get on with life – but some become noticeably silent about everything, and for a time are underachieving.

Other teenagers just can't cope with this burden which has been imposed on them involuntarily. They try to eradicate it from their minds, endeavouring to behave as though nothing has happened – with a poor outlook for later life, when they will have to deal with other difficulties. Others start to go along the slippery road of drugs, alcohol or sex for consolation and oblivion. In his desperate longing for comfort and understanding, more than one boy has turned to an older girl and then found himself in the compounded situation of being the father of her child, thus perpetuating the scenario of a child without a home.

Some children know that they were born as a result

of their parents' (often misguided) attempt to keep the marriage together. This places an inappropriate weight of responsibility on their young shoulders. If, after all their efforts, the parents do eventually separate, the children's sense of failure and guilt is enormous.

Not only divorce

Of course, divorce is not the only affliction which children have to bear. Physical divorce is sometimes almost easier than the emotional divorce which exists between two parents who live in the same house but are constantly fighting or maintaining a frigid silence, or who have such an unsatisfactory relationship that the children become abused in one way or another. Many children have no real home life, even if their parents are not actually living apart; there may be enough money, but no affection, no family life, and no sense of belonging. An atmosphere of warm affection and emotional security is essential for healthy emotional growth both during the foundational years of early childhood and during the turbulent days of adolescence. Material possessions are of secondary importance.

We see all around us people who are carrying great internal wounds inflicted by their parents' marriage and/or divorce. For parents, divorce is usually the *symptom* of a deeper trouble, but for children the marital disharmony can be one of the basic *causes* of their troubles. These children are the parents of the next generation. They carry the future in their hands. Some suffer more than others, but all children of divorce and marital disturbance do suffer.

Sometimes I am asked to help with selection interviewing for a society with which I am involved.

When I read the papers of the candidates I always heave a sigh of relief when I read the words, 'I was brought up in a loving, united home, and still have a warm and close relationship with both my parents.' Those candidates are always the ones who seem to be stable and well integrated, able to bear the stresses of life with less likelihood of collapsing under the strain. Their foundations have been laid securely.

Divorce or death?

Divorce is not the only reason for family break-ups, of course. There is the cruel hand of death, which disrupts the harmony of a family and leaves its members shattered, bewildered, angry and confused, sometimes on a long-term basis. Death of a parent may cause great grief, loneliness and sorrow, but at least it is 'clean', in that there is not the implied statement to the child that the departing parent prefers to live with someone other than that child. There is no constant reminder that the parent is around somewhere and might be encountered again in circumstances which might be difficult to handle. Death leaves many painful issues – sometimes anger and confusion; certainly sadness and longings – but not so many jagged edges.

Research shows clearly that losing a parent through death has a less adverse effect on children's subsequent life-course and transition into adulthood than experiencing the breakdown of their parents' marriage. The disruption is very important, but the *cause* of the disruption matters more.

Internal pressures in a marriage

The dynamics which operate between two people in a marriage relationship are complex and specific to that partnership. The individuals have to struggle with their own longing for intimacy and yet also with the fear of being engulfed. Fusion, like separation, can bring the fear of losing oneself. They also have to adjust to the changes in their own level of maturity over the years as it interacts with the changes in the spouse's level. In addition, the presence of real children in the household activates the 'child' which lives on in every adult. The couple have to work together and individually with their respective emotional neediness and confusion, letting go some preconceived certainties and ideas which previously had seemed so assured, and learning to understand and value the different 'language' that the other speaks. Forgiveness often means staying with the pain and working at it, when it would be much easier to escape or to dig one's heels in about the rightness of one's own position.

When each partner has considered his or her own 'rights to self-fulfilment' and personal growth, there are other important issues, such as responsibility, fidelity and commitment to the marriage and the children. These are often great areas of conflict and perceived threat, requiring much maturity from both partners to stay with and work at the difficulties when unilateral declarations of independence seem tempting. Nothing is easy or simple.

In her courageous and moving foreword to a biography of Dr Frank Lake, Sylvia, his widow and the mother of their three children, says:

> I struggled to love Frank; sometimes it was
> very difficult to love him, yet for me it was
> an unbreakable bond of love. Sometimes it
> seemed as though he deliberately tried to
> destroy love, as though to prove once and

for all that love was a fallacy. Of course, I failed over and over again. But I believed in love, knew from whence comes the love that does not fail us and held on firmly to God even when it seemed that all the ground had been kicked from beneath my feet. Archimandrite Sophrony speaks of the experience of the hell of love. These words have meaning for me. I do not think anyone would have called our house a peaceful place to be in those days. Yet I see now that the great battles of humanity were being lived out there in our tiny environment; the battles of the heart, the battle of love versus selfishness and self-centredness; the battle between light and darkness; the battle between life and death. And that is exactly how it is for every one of us here – now – in this paltry little back street, with these sordid emotions, and tears of self-pity and of glory . . . Cost there was. Yet, in God's plan it became a means of grace, a crucible without which I would not have been where I am today . . . It is as we go *through* the little deaths that resurrection follows. 'Be ye faithful unto death, and I will give you a crown of life.'[2]

The rhythms of marriage

As the years go by, there are natural rhythms in the marriage. There are the early years when achieving is the main preoccupation – career-building and the raising of children. Then come the middle years when the children are wanting to build their own lives and leave home, and career advancement for the parents takes a different perspective. The husband is beginning to want his creature comforts and to return more to home, and at that time his wife may be wanting to spread her wings and spend less time at home. Both, in their different ways, are saying, 'What is life all about?' Then there are the later years, when the couple are thrown together much more and work no longer has its distancing advantages. Physical and financial limitations may be an important new factor to encompass in mutual forebearance.

These are among the internal factors which operate in the developing relationship between husband and wife. Many people do adjust their original expectations of marriage, achieve some of their ideals, contain their disappointments, grow up a bit, learn how to handle conflict, adapt to changing circumstances, and manage to work out enough satisfaction to maintain a loving, forgiving and mutually enriching relationship, through better and worse. Clulow and Mattinson comment:

> To love and be loved so that, despite failing, each is the most precious person in the world to the other even after forty or fifty years, can be one of the highest of human achievements and the greatest of satisfactions. Marriage then matters most importantly, because it is a statement that we, as individuals, matter.[3]

External pressures on a marriage

In addition to all the internal factors, there are pressures that arise from the outside world: unemployment, inadequate housing, redundancy, ill-health, financial stringency, pressure from family or friends. The current climate in society generally can impose great stress on a marriage and its children at the same time as the internal dynamics are operating. Magazines, newspapers, films, radio and television have a very formative influence in defining the culture in which two people conduct their marriage. (Buckmaster Fuller is said to have forecast some years ago that television would become 'a third parent' in terms of influence.) In our contemporary Western culture the emphasis is on individual human rights and self-fulfilment. These priorities have been promoted over and above any commitment and faithfulness to the marriage and to the partner, to children and other relatives. People are not encouraged to work at their problems. Divorce is now regarded as a normal and acceptable escape from a situation which does not offer maximum personal gratification.

Public concern

If marriage is one of life's major events, so is divorce. A marriage becomes a matter of public concern at its inception and also when it breaks down. People feel ill at ease and distressed when they hear that their friends are divorcing. A broken marriage imposes change on many lives in addition to the participants of the marriage. Confusions and disruption follow, with changed relationships. A domino effect can sometimes be observed among a group of friends when one couple splits up.

Public distress is at its height when children are involved. How will they manage? How will it affect them in the present and in the long term? The *Sunday Times* of 13 December 1992 published a piece about a ten-year-old boy, William, whose parents had separated very recently. It said:

Despite his public image as a boisterous tearaway, he is like his father – reserved and shy. Mature for his age, he is 'quite formal and stiff'. He is very protective of his mother, hugging and kissing her at every opportunity, and worrying about her when she is unhappy, which ... is most of the time. As with all pre-adolescents, he is extremely sensitive to his parents' situation. He is finding it hard to understand why 'papa' ... has not done more to 'protect his mother' [from the unhappiness]. Over the past year he has become noticeably more introverted ... he is quieter than he used to be, preferring his own company or the company of adults to that of his contemporaries.

William's father had had long periods of separation from his own parents because of their work. His mother, as a vulnerable young girl, had experienced the trauma of her mother leaving the matrimonial home. Now the miserable experience of family break-up was being passed on to William, despite all efforts to soften the blow.

Grandparents are also deeply affected, because they often have a very special and important relationship with their grandchildren, and their contact may be weakened as a result of the disrupted family. The children, also, may be grieved by the loss of grandparents and confused by the unwanted arrival of another set of grandparents.

So the sorry story of divorce has to be admitted. When the bough breaks the cradle falls; down comes baby, cradle and all.

15

The Bible, children and divorce

Whether we like it or not, we are part of twentieth-century Western society, with its confusion and instability all around us. Christians have been caught up in this culture and often accept its values uncritically. We are influenced, imperceptibly, by the highlighting of the breakdown of other people's marriages and by the easy acceptance of infidelity and broken relationships. We are not immune to problems in our own marriages. We, ourselves, may be tempted to be unfaithful to our spouses. We suffer from our own compulsive need to control things and people. We envy one another and are quick to feel rejection.

How do we find our way through the maze of our own personal emotional needs and relationships? Are we free to exercise our individual rights and 'do our own thing'? Do changing moral fashions affect the way we Christians live our lives? Do we agree that the only course of action, if distress arises within the marriage relationship, is to terminate it? That is certainly the wisdom of this world, but does it have validity for the followers of Jesus, who are invited to reflect God's image in the quality of their relationships? A Christian woman of fifty-six said recently, 'We are thinking of getting a divorce. At one time we wouldn't have thought about it, but it doesn't seem to matter so much now.'

What has happened to God's will when things work out badly? How do we know what God's will is, anyway? Can we apply biblical thinking to the confusions of the modern world, to our attitudes to marriage, to divorce, to the care of our children, to the rights of the individual, and to personal relationships? How can we find some guidelines to help us find our way through the maze of modern opinions?

Some guidelines

Certainly, the Christian will not make his or her moral choices on the basis that 'everyone does it' or 'it seemed a good idea at the time'. Neither will the decisions be made solely on the observable facts of the situation or on hopes of what will produce the greatest happiness and personal fulfilment in the long run.

The Bible

The practising Christian looks to the Bible and the Holy Spirit for guidelines. Some people use a very literal approach to the text of Scripture; but this presents difficulties over the subjects about which the Bible has nothing to say, such as abortion, contraception, transplant surgery, genetic engineering, Aids, the nuclear family and so on. There are specific guidelines about some things, but it would have been

172

impossible for the biblical writers to have been specific about everything, because cultures differ, fashions change, and knowledge increases. This leads other people at the opposite end of the scale to deduce that the Bible has *nothing* relevant to say to our modern generation. It is true that life in the modern world may seem to be more complex than it was in those far-off days when there were fewer choices.

Both these views fail to understand what sort of book the Bible is. It comes to us as God's revelation about what sort of a God he is, about the world and human beings. These facts are no less true because they are conveyed in a culturally conditioned form. (Compare, on a lesser scale, the fact that we are constantly amazed at Shakespeare's penetrating insight into human nature and do not baulk at the fact that his plays were written in Elizabethan English in the culture of 300 years ago!) The cultural difference does not mean that the Bible is irrelevant to us. It means that we have to apply ourselves to careful interpretation, taking single passages in the light of the whole and trying to interpret the meaning of the authors in the light of our own situation, so that the word which God spoke in that way at that time will speak to us today.

In the Bible, therefore, we have basic guidelines which fit the human condition in general, and which are applicable to all people in all places and in all times. We need the wisdom of God's Holy Spirit to help us to apply these guidelines appropriately to our situation.

The special relationship with God

The whole story of the Bible in both the Old and New Testaments is about the special, personal relationship of God with his people: the permanent covenant which he made with them; his costly, committed love for them, and his yearning that it should be a reciprocal relationship. This was to be an on-going relationship of growing depth and trust; that is why God refers to it so many times as a marriage, or to himself as a father or mother. This was a covenant, not merely of involvement but commitment. (In a totally different context, General Norman Schwarzkopf once said: 'Imagine a bacon-and-egg breakfast. The chicken is involved but the pig is committed.') The sad tale of how this relationship was broken, with its damaging results, is a recurring biblical theme. The ancient prophets used to bewail the infidelity of the people in the colourful language of marriage and divorce. Infidelity had never been God's intention, though he had plenty of cause to terminate the covenant.

Furthermore, this special relationship of loving and personal trust was intended to be a primary demonstration about the nature of God to the peoples adjacent to Israel, whose way of life did not include a personal relationship of this sort. In one of his letters, however, Paul had to confront the Jews (God's special people) with the horrible accusation: 'God's name is blasphemed among the Gentiles because of you' (Rom. 2:24).

The special relationship with one another

One of the results of this loving relationship with God is that relationships between human beings follow the same direction. So we find all the commandments encapsulated by Jesus thus: 'Love the Lord your God with all your heart and with all your soul and with all your mind . . . Love your neighbour as yourself' (Mt. 22:37, 39). Indeed, the apostle John goes so far as to say: 'Anyone who does not love his brother, whom he has seen, cannot love God, whom

174

he has not seen' (1 Jn. 4:20). (Alas, it is often much easier to 'love' people we cannot see! But perhaps that is the whole point of John's statement.) A legal contract is specific, exact and particular, deliberately designed to restrict room for manoeuvre. A covenant, on the other hand, allows room for and encourages growth within it. For Christians, the marriage ceremony is itself both a legal contract and a covenant before God, in addition to being a reflection of God's covenant love to us.

The special relationship with the children

We have spent a great deal of time thinking about the importance of relationships to children. We have considered that one purpose of the family is to teach children about the nature of God and to create an atmosphere in which he is a credible reality. The whole tenor of Scripture agrees.

There are actually few explicit biblical references to broken homes and their implications for children. But the one in Malachi 2:10–16 is unambiguous. The prophet is speaking to the children of Israel about their heart-attitude to their God in relation to the covenant. He is also reminding them of the picture of God that they are painting for the surrounding Godless people by their behaviour.

> Why do we profane the covenant of our fathers by breaking faith with one another? . . .
>
> You flood the LORD's altar with tears. You weep and wail because he no longer pays attention to your offerings or accepts them with pleasure from your hands. You ask, 'Why?' It is because the LORD is acting as the witness between you and the wife of your

youth, because you have broken faith with her, though she is your partner, the wife of your marriage covenant.

Has not the LORD made them one? In flesh and spirit they are his. And why one? *Because he was seeking godly offspring.* So guard yourself in your spirit, and do not break faith with the wife of your youth.

'I hate divorce,' says the LORD God of Israel, 'and I hate a man's covering himself with violence as well as with his garment,' says the LORD Almighty.

So guard yourself in your spirit, and do not break faith.[1]

In commenting on this verse, Joyce Baldwin says that God sees divorce as like *covering one's garment with violence.* This is a figurative expression for all kinds of gross injustice which, like the blood of a murdered victim, leave their mark for all to see.[2]

Not only is the covenant of the love relationship severed, with all the attendant confusion and distress, when there is persistent parental disaffection, but the prototype for the children has been destroyed. What sort of a picture of God do children get when they cannot rely safely on their parents? ('Why did Jesus have to make this happen to us?') Not only do love and trust in other people become difficult, but the children begin to wonder whether they themselves are lovable. This does not sound much like 'godly offspring'.

Jesus himself put it even more directly, if that were possible: 'Woe betide the man through whom [causes of stumbling] come. It would be better for him to be thrown into the sea with a millstone round his neck than to cause one of these little ones to stumble. Keep watch on yourselves' (Lk. 17:2–3, NEB).

In view of all that we know about parents being a signpost or representative of God to their children, this is a very serious warning indeed. Perhaps the greatest indictment against us at the end of the twentieth century is that so much knowledge is available about the emotional needs and development of children and the subsequent spiritual awareness built on that, but so little notice is taken of that knowledge. In our determined search for self-fulfilment and individualism it is usually the children who have to pay the price: in our half-hearted commitment to them, they learn not to commit themselves totally to anyone or anything unless it suits their own purposes. They often learn that 'loving' means 'leaving', and that is too painful. It does not take too much observation to discover that the unreliability of parents and of loving family life is one of the causes of widespread confusion and corruption in our society generally. We cannot stress often enough that *parental disturbance makes the inner world of a child very insecure.*

Commitment means sticking with the situation, somehow containing the pain, disloyalty or misunderstanding, finding a way of living with difficulties and distress, looking for more effective ways of communicating, and not throwing in the towel when the going gets tough – as it is bound to, from time to time. Here we have a very basic guideline. Commitment, faithfulness and permanence determine decisions about marriage, divorce, cohabitation, the care of children and the awareness of their emotional needs. Genuine love depends not on the response we receive but on the degree of commitment. Love is the most difficult thing to practise. Eroticism and gratification come easily to us, but not love, with its rigorous implications. This has nothing to do with the soft, sentimental and indulgent image of love which is so prevalent today. It is about unconditional commitment, for better or for worse, when things are exciting and when they are difficult, with no ending clause. Nothing can part us from the love of God – neither death, nor life, nor anything else (Rom. 8:38–39). This is the stuff of which love is made, in which God invites us to participate. Such love is tough as well as tender, uncomfortable and uncompromising as well as comforting, forgiving and full of compassion.

When it does not work

In Martin Luther's robust words, 'Ah, dear God, marriage is not a thing of nature but a gift of God: the sweetest, the dearest, and the purest life . . . when it turns out well, though the very devil if it does not.' The basic assumption of the world around us, dictated and mediated largely through television and the media, says, 'Anything goes;' 'Everyone does it;' 'It's all right as long as no-one gets hurt;' 'It's my own private business – nothing to do with anyone else;' 'I must fulfil myself;' 'We have fallen out of love;' 'I want it, so I'll have it.' For a Christian there are more important considerations. In the light of our guidelines, casual divorce for an insubstantial reason is seen to be totally inappropriate.

But how can we go on loving and living when we are constantly rejected, misunderstood, persistently devalued or ignored and possibly physically abused? Can we still continue in faithful commitment? It must be said that in some cases divorce appears to be the only option when all else has failed. It is true that divorce may bring an end to some of the active problems, but a marriage can never be expunged, even for couples who have no children. Divorce never solves everything completely: it usually opens the door to a different set of problems.

In view of the guidelines we have been discovering, it would seem that a Christian should be very careful indeed before initiating a divorce, unless there are extreme circumstances of mental or physical danger because of gross cruelty. If an application for divorce is being made against him or her, there might be grounds for contesting it because of the 'covenant' aspect. This would depend on whether the couple had had adequate counselling from a professional therapist or a wise and experienced older Christian before the decision to part. Certainly, no definite steps to break a marriage should ever be taken without careful counselling for both parties.

There are times when a new relationship has been entered into before the formal termination of the old one. Obviously, this complicates and influences decisions. The serious and premature inclusion of a third party indicates that some of the guidelines have already become blurred. The guidelines are about commitment and faithfulness to the spouse and the children despite whatever provocation, as a reflection of the seriousness of God's covenant with us. *Marriage is not something that can be discarded when it becomes inconvenient.*

If a breakdown of the relationship is really irreparable despite genuine efforts at reconciliation and understanding, it is important to struggle seriously with feelings of bitterness and recrimination and not to play the 'blame game'. It takes two to make a quarrel, and there is seldom a 'guilty party', though one partner may act out the difficulties more than the other. It is easy to talk about forgiveness: it is another thing to practise it. Forgiveness is not just a few kindly, and usually costly, words. It is a lifestyle. We do well to recall the attitude of Jesus when he said: 'Forgive us our sins as we forgive them who sin against us.'

It is unwise to lay down hard-and-fast rules about when and when not to divorce. Everybody's circumstances are different, and God is not a God of rules. However, the undergirding principle of it all is *love*. The warmth and enthusiasm of love have usually died when a marriage is at an end, but it is still possible to show love in the way divorce proceedings and the subsequent negotiations are conducted. In this situation, love is demonstrated by fighting fairly, considering the welfare of the partner and the children, not being unscrupulous, and not harbouring grudges in spite of the injuries and injustices which may have been inflicted. That is sometimes a hard assignment.

Acceptance

Divorce in circumstances such as adultery was acknowledged from the earliest days, because that implied a broken covenant. The meticulous regulations stipulated in the Old Testament were for the protection both of the people involved and of society generally. Even though divorce was not God's will, there was no question of either party being ostracized or remaining unloved and unforgiven, if they were open to love. Had such a situation prevailed, it would have been in contradiction to the whole of the nature of the God of love.

There are occasions, sadly, when the divorce has taken place against the will of one of the partners. Whatever the circumstances, however, it is possible that out of all the pain, self-discovery, and deep examination of the issues, growth can occur; sometimes the personal shell has to be broken so that a potential chicken can emerge. Even from the most distressing circumstances some benefits can be found, but, alas, in the case of divorce, the growth of the adults may be at the price of damage to the children.

16

Preventing the hurts

'So,' you might say, 'now we know what causes childhood hurts and subsequent adult problems, but how do we prevent them?'

It might be too simplistic to reply, 'If you don't want explosions, don't plant time bombs.'

Anti-terrorist police have two main objectives in view. One is to find the terrorists, the other is to blockade the supply routes. Sometimes the police have huge successes after months of intensive investigation and patient work. The motivation behind all this effort is that they are aware of the enormous potential damage to people and to property, with all the attendant emotional and physical cost. But terrorists are usually determined, resourceful and difficult to catch. We have a similarly difficult task on hand if we are trying to stem the escalation in broken homes, single-parent families and their ensuing devastation of human lives.

What can we do?

We have looked at length at some of the residual problems for which healing is needed: disruption of the inner emotional world, feelings of guilt, shame, unresolved grief, inability to trust or make commitments, or to make satisfying relationships at a deep level, and so on. There are also problems for society and for the church at large which need to be examined in order to set a healthier climate for marriage in which breakdown is less likely to happen. It is really more constructive to consider how to prevent divorce by reinforcing marriage than to think about what can be done to heal the wounds after the event. Let's think if there is some contribution we can make to help the situation.

Recognition

On the whole, we are becoming lulled into a sense of complacency about broken homes. They are so common and seem almost unavoidable, so we throw up our hands in helpless dismay and become resigned to inevitability. Everyone knows that a broken home is an inadequate place for a child to grow up in, in spite of the voices which become loud in defensive protest. We do not really need research projects to prove what everyone's eyes can see. They merely confirm the known facts with depressing statistics.

It is *not* acceptable simply to submit to this state of affairs. (That is not to say that we should not accept the people within these situations.) As human beings, not to mention as Christians, how can we stand aside and see this tragedy which is engulfing our society and not feel responsible in some way? The size of the problem is immeasurable, and growing fast.

Education

There seems to be a great unwillingness to be serious about the emotional needs of small children and the importance of the foundational relationships which have such an impact on later life in marriage and other relationships. We need to alert parents to their contribution to a child's emotional and spiritual well-being. How many times have I heard people say, 'Why didn't anyone tell us about it? We never knew!'

183

There is no excuse for people not to know, now, in this modern age. Whether we like what we hear is another matter, because it attacks the cult of individualism, which we have come to regard as our right. Sometimes it seems as though we have not progressed much beyond the stage of Cain, one of the earliest Bible characters, who asked with some defiance, 'Am I my brother's keeper?' We need to remember the point which I will repeat because it is so important: the central focus of the Bible's view of family is not on the institution but on *the quality of personal relationships* within it.

How are we to improve those relationships? You may recall that the first vital foundation stones in building relationships are laid in the early months and years of life. Some of us have opportunities to pass on some education in order that people can no longer say, 'Why were we never told?'

Opportunities do exist. We may have formal contact with young parents – for example, at mothers' and toddlers' groups – and we could play an important part in helping them to understand what is involved in the emotional development of children and the implications of parenting. Church leaders have a big task here, too, and are often ill equipped to understand what makes people tick, how they get into the difficulties that arise and how to address them. It is not enough to urge people to pray about it unless their prayers have been directed helpfully. Sermons need to be related to the whole person, helping us to grow in humanness, which, of course, includes spirituality. We cannot find God until we have found ourselves, for God's dwelling-place is in our heart. One of the reasons so many people do not bother with church-going or Christianity is that it is not seen to be relevant to their lives. What an indictment!

The church has a tremendous privilege and responsibility here. It could be at the forefront of the battle to try to enlarge and preserve the emotional and spiritual lives of children and adults.

Divorce and a broken home are not evils which the partners perpetrate deliberately because of their badness. It is an evil arising from various emotional deprivations and consequent negative interactions which the partners bring to their marriage and about which the majority have little understanding. And then the 'sins' of the parents are visited on the children from one generation to another – 'the cycle of deprivation'. Part of the church's task, as David Atkinson says, is 'to help people to develop the sort of characters which are capable of making and sustaining relationships, honouring obligations, showing love and being faithful'.[1] The church family can create a 'facilitating environment' by its loving, accepting warmth, and its example, especially for the people whose early years have been damaged. Some of them may be picked up in Junior Church or youth groups.

Marriage preparation

One of the huge problem areas is the lack of shared understanding about the nature of marriage. As we know, some people rush into it with only the haziest notion of what they are doing, and with impossible expectations of what it will deliver. We would do well to remember the sonorous introduction to the marriage service in the *Book of Common Prayer*, which reads:

> Holy Matrimony ... is not by any to be
> interprised, nor taken in hand, unadvisedly,
> lightly, or wantonly, to satisfy men's carnal

lusts and appetites, like brute beasts that
have no understanding; but reverently, dis-
creetly, advisedly, soberly, and in the fear of
God; duly considering the causes for which
Matrimony was ordained.

We seem to have forgotten that, in these days of
'enlightenment'! We need a greatly increased awareness of what marriage is and what it is not.

We also need to be reminded constantly that marriage *per se* will not deliver satisfying relationships
automatically. The church's task is to teach people
about the nature of marriage and help them to avoid
the absurdly high expectations that lead to disappointment in marriage and family relationships.

Marriage preparation begins at birth, when the
small child is taking in the atmosphere in which he
lives and absorbing the way the parents relate, or fail
to relate, to each other and to him in love, in anger
and in the 'nothing special' times.

The easiest time to begin marriage preparation
informally is in the youth groups, before any serious
commitments are made. Once the couple have made
up their minds that this is what they want to do, they
are less able to consider the issues dispassionately. It
is important to have discussions, either as a group or
privately, about relationships: what they involve;
expectations; models that they would like to copy;
how to communicate positively; how to argue con-
structively; how to listen effectively to what the other
person is saying, and so on. Leaders of such groups
need to equip themselves adequately to do this, by
reading or talking with people who could help them
or by inviting outside people to lead discussions,
although it is easier for the young to be open with the
leaders they know. Sometimes these matters, which

are of paramount interest and relevance to the young, are dodged, over-spiritualized or simply omitted.

The amount of official preparation for marriage that is done in many churches leaves much to be desired. When we think of the enormous undertaking on which these two people are embarking, it should be a *priority* task for the church. It is a primary outreach post, too, because all sorts of people come to be married in church, whether or not they have any Christian commitment.

It need not be done by the church staff, necessarily, because most ministers have enough to do. Ordinary members of the church community can do it if they are suitable and are fired by the importance of the task. There is some extremely good and flexible material (information, suggestions, videos, checklists, *etc.*) available to guide and help the inexperienced, the faint-hearted and the timorous.[2]

On the whole, at this point in their lives, people tend to welcome more insight into what makes healthy relationships and what working at them involves, such as effective listening to each other, handling conflict productively and fighting fairly (rather than indulging in 'the blame game'). Most people go into their own marriage knowing that many marriages do break down, but hoping their own will not, although not necessarily knowing how to prevent it happening. They marry, largely unaware that each person takes into marriage some emotional luggage (such as jealousy, fear of anger, and experiences of rejection). They will be faced with this luggage in the intimacy and the continuous contact of marriage. What are they to do with it? They may need to think about what each may feel like when the first baby arrives. They probably have no idea that a threesome feels quite different from a twosome.

These sorts of issues are really more valuable than talks on finance and sex, though they have a place; that information is readily available elsewhere. We are interested, primarily, in helping couples to engage with deeper emotional realities which are the foundation for their relationship. It is very helpful to give them a checklist to fill in separately so that they can discover how well they think they know each other, what their emotional and sexual needs are and the sort of problems they might anticipate. It is not usually the known difficulties that cause the greatest problems, but the unknown ones. If a person has major difficulties before the marriage, however, he or she will almost certainly have them afterwards.

The couple who take their marriage seriously are usually grateful for the opportunity to think together about some areas of their relationship which they had not considered, or some fears that they had not thought sufficiently important, or had the courage, to express. They might talk about their parental model and what that implies for their own marriage. Sue Walrond-Skinner writes: 'Each of the pair has to separate sufficiently from their families of origin to enable them to engage in their new relationship . . . and to leave behind bondage to past expectations and experiences.'[3] At the same time their marriage will be a bonding between the two families.

The scope is wide. The couples who come to church to be married are offering us a unique opportunity to be involved in their budding relationship, but we fail to take advantage of it. This might be one of the occasions when they would welcome some discussion about the relevance of the living Jesus Christ in personal relationships.

There is no point in taking a negative view of divorce if we do not do our utmost to create positive conditions to enable marriage to survive. Some people will not take their marriage preparation seriously, but that does not absolve us from our responsibility to offer them thought-provoking opportunities.

Preparation for a second marriage is very important. Whereas on the first occasion it might be educative in value, in the second it may be more therapeutic. In every case, attention must be paid to understanding and resolving past difficulties and to healing the hurts as well as looking at the new expectations.

Marriage enrichment

One young woman who had been married for a year said, 'You can't prepare people for marriage, but they certainly need to be cared for afterwards!' – especially during those first years, when disillusionment is high. Much help has been received by many people from the better marriage enrichment movements. The participants are invited to go on a weekend away from their domestic commitments and are helped to assess where they are at that moment in their growth together and how they could improve their sensitivity to each other. They are not expected to make embarrassing disclosures unless they want to. The object of the exercise is for the couples themselves to improve their own relationship together, not to edify spectators.

Watchfulness

Ourselves

Most of the biblical references in our chapter on divorce ended with some injunction such as 'So guard yourself in your spirit . . .' (Mal. 2:16) and 'So watch yourselves' (Lk. 17:2). Don't we need to be much less casual about our Christian lives and the influence of the external things we watch or read? We need to walk closely with the Lord and spend deliberate time communicating internally with him, just as we would in marriage. If we can understand our own needs and weaknesses we need not become a prey to our inner drives. We may have become Christians, but that does not mean that we lose our natural emotional deformities and deprivations immediately. We need to understand our deeper motivations and have the courage to face them.

Roger was a lay reader; he did a great deal of preaching and was punctilious about his 'quiet time'. The whole of his family went to church regularly. But he was cold and distant in his relationships with his family and said he had never been good at relation-ships. When Roger was a small child of four, he had had the dreadful separation experience of being evacuated during the war, without his family. He had not understood about bombs and danger; he had only known that he didn't know where he was, who he was with or where his parents were. When he was five he was sent to boarding-school. In order to sur-vive he learnt to acquire a very stiff upper lip so that his tender emotions would not overwhelm him. It is not difficult to understand that as an adult, intimate relationships were difficult and painful for him. He was afraid to trust himself to anyone for fear of re-experiencing the childhood pain which was so deeply buried that it could not be articulated.

When Roger eventually left his wife to live with another woman, after various incidents of infidelity, he told his daughter, Katherine, 'I've never been a Christian.' Roger had been overwhelmed by his intense inner need for love, which had never been acknowledged and faced or perhaps even understood. He was stuck emotionally at the level of a four-year-old, despite his considerable business acumen, and was searching for a degree of warmth and love which he could not find, in spite of his various affairs. Neither could he find it in God, despite all his efforts.

There are a great many Rogers around. We cannot excuse ourselves just because we have been hurt in the past, though that may be the fundamental reason for our distress. We must 'guard our spirits' in the present and make every effort to see that the deep, hidden needs which surface so inconveniently are met appropriately so that they do not overwhelm us eventually.

Other people

Roger's son Ben was outraged by all this. He threw the whole 'church-going business' out of the window. Not surprisingly, he regarded it as 'all a load of hypocrisy', particularly as the other woman also 'called herself a Christian'. To this day Ben has not had anything more to do with the church.

'No man is an island, entire of itself . . .' We are accountable for our brothers and sisters.

One of the first evidences of evil in the world was broken relationships: the relationships between God and his created friends, between the man and his wife, and within the personal inner world of the people themselves. The story has continued all down the centuries and nothing much has changed – except that God did intervene in order to restore relationships. Surely the Christian message of love and forgiveness is utterly relevant at the point of people's needs. Could we work on this so that those people who have no time for 'the church-going business' will see the relevance of our gradual growth into mature humanness as it was originally intended, or as Jesus Christ displayed it?

Our responsibility for others also includes being watchful for people who may be struggling in their relationships, praying for them, being approachable so that they feel safe to talk if they wish to, listening attentively to them and supporting them in whatever way is appropriate and sensitive. It may seem intrusive to enquire about the state of someone's marriage; certainly it is not normal polite practice! But there are ways of doing it less directly, without causing embarrassment. It is surprising how people welcome a listening ear (and a silent tongue!).

Knowing ourselves

Katherine and Ben's mother was an affectionate woman who had married with idealized expectations of romantic love, but had soon discovered that 'everything was flat'. Katherine was thirteen when Roger left the family home, saying to her, 'Don't worry. This won't affect you.' (How little did he know about relationships and love!) Actually, it had been quite a relief when he went, because there had been so much tension. But it was hard for Katherine to accept the other woman with whom he went to live. Although Ben just dismissed Roger and all he represented, Katherine was still yearning for every teenage girl's first lover – her father. She was sixteen when her parents actually divorced.

When her father chose to leave her in favour of someone else, the realization that this woman was more important than she was too painful to bear. He had never really listened to her and was always hidden behind the newspaper. The other woman underlined for Katherine the fact that 'I wasn't necessary in his life'. Her self-confidence received a tremendous blow. The new woman seemed to be setting high standards with which Katherine felt she could not possibly compete. She could not confront her Dad and ask him questions because he was always in the new woman's house. Also, she felt a very deep sense of humiliation because they all lived in the same village and her shame was public.

When Katherine herself became a Christian, she was greatly helped by the awareness that she was loved and accepted by God. This seemed to calm her fears and hurt to some extent, but she still had this great yearning for her father's love and attention. Although she knew in her head that the family had been split irrevocably, Roger was still her father and her heart was still saying, 'What would Dad think of this?' and 'How can I make him proud of me? He isn't proud of me, so I must achieve, in order to get his attention.'

And so her life went on, in a miserable sequence of not finding what she was seeking, in spite of her mother's various attempts at encouragement. Her mother had also been rejected by this man who was so important to her, so was her mother really a good guide?

Eventually, at the age of twenty-one, Katherine married a man who was considerably older than she, a man who had known problems in his own emotional life, whom she soon found to be mean and cruel, and with whom there was a total breakdown in communication. Within two years she too was divorced. History was repeating itself in her attempt to find her father by replacing him.

As Katherine grew in her Christian life, she came to realize that her anger against her father was preventing her both from finding herself and from finding God; she needed release from the revenge, the bitterness and the perpetual thought that 'if it hadn't been for you, I would not be like this'. She began to think about forgiveness. It was difficult. She had made many attempts to get in touch with her father (who now lived abroad permanently), but without response. She was still 'on her high horse' about it, angry about his silence and resenting the fact that he did not make the first moves in her direction. She began to see that her own attitude was not helping, so she began to wait for a great surge of love to come into her heart instead of the resentment; but nothing happened.

Since the end of her own marriage, Katherine has not had any men in her life, although she is attractive and still in her twenties. She avoids potential involvements now, 'although my friends go in and out of friendships and marriage quite easily and they think I am strange'. Katherine knows in her head a lot about the idea of 'unconditional love', but she finds it a very difficult concept to take on board emotionally. She cannot see that at the root of everything, she is still unwilling to abandon her efforts to hold Roger as the ideal parent in her internal fantasy world.

Until she is willing to let her ideal fantasy father go and accept her real father as he is, she will not be able to forgive in any thoroughgoing way. The pain of loss will not necessarily end then, because she has actually been let down, but the resentment and bitterness will vanish. She will be able to live without looking over her shoulder all the time for the father who does not come. That is forgiveness, and that is the way to finding herself, finding God, and finding the nourishing love in other relationships which she so sorely needs.

It is not always easy for us to see exactly what is happening under the surface, but when some unhappiness is eating away and preventing us from making progress in one area or another, it is time to look for someone who can help us.

Sources of help

People often need expert help when they are trying to work out the problems in their marriage, and they need not be ashamed to ask for it. It is not a failure to recognize that one is out of one's depth, and to call for help. Organizations such as Relate and the Institute for Marital Studies are designed to help people to understand what is happening in their own personal lives and in their marriage. Unfortunately, there is a false notion abroad in some sections of the church that Christians should not need this sort of assistance. So, unhappily, people are inhibited from using the resources that the Holy Spirit has made available – in addition to prayer.

Help for the children

The manner in which a child is told about the break-up of the family, and the person who tells him, are immensely important. Although the child may be aware of tension and unhappiness, he does not want to believe that his own home is about to become a casualty. Some parents, realizing that it will be a terrible blow to the child, prefer to leave it to someone else to break the news. This is hard for the child. The parents have inflicted the blow, he thinks to himself, and they should be the ones to tell him about it. The confusion is compounded in his mind if he is just left to find out or deduce that things have changed. This can lead to all sorts of bitterness.

The transition to a step-family is almost as difficult as the break-up of the original family unit. Comments such as, 'Go away. You're not my Daddy,' from a young child, and 'We've got a mum, thanks. We don't need you,' from an older child, indicate the strength of feeling that can exist. The step-parents also have their problems.

All children need a friendly adult outside the family in whom to confide. Often, for junior-school children, this will be the teacher; but it could be the Brownie or Cub pack leader, or one of the helpers in the Junior Church. But a child will tell only someone whom he feels to be understanding and kind and with whom there is some sort of relationship. In a large comprehensive school, where pupils move from classroom to classroom, there is often less chance for teachers to observe their pupils intimately; so the need, although as great, is less easily met. They need someone, other than their contemporaries, for consolation, and yet they may be less spontaneous. A sympathetic, non-critical, impartial confidante who is just quietly available as a sounding-board can be an invaluable support while the child mourns the loss of a parent and possibly a home as well.

Without the proper facilities for mourning, much unhealthy feeling will be pushed under the carpet, waiting to explode at a later date. The loss of parents must be grieved and felt, not repressed or denied. It must be worked through. But the grieving cannot be done in isolation; ideally it should be with another person who will offer comfort and acceptance. Sadness may always be there, but forgiveness and healing eventually take the place of anger and hurt when there has been adequate grieving. Forgiveness means working at these things.

Rosemary Wells offers a great deal of practical

wisdom on this point in her book *Helping Children Cope with Divorce*. As a negative example, she quotes Christine, who put her trust in her art teacher. 'I though she would be sympathetic. Instead, she started telling me what to do – things like understanding mum, how women need to express themselves and how dad would learn from looking after me. Nothing about *me*, or *my* feelings. I wished I had kept quiet.'[4]

The church community

Jill was the third of four children. When she was nine she went into her mother's bedroom to have her hair plaited, and her parents snapped at each other. When Jill protested, her father said, 'Don't worry: your Mum and I are going to separate.'

Jill felt shocked, cheated and deceived, because she had thought they were a happy family. But she remembered lying in bed and listening to her mother sitting on the stairs having long and unhappy phone conversations. She did not know why. She thought they were a respectable family and no-one would have believed what was going on. It would have been easier for her to accept if there had been obvious disarray.

Jill felt, very painfully, that she was not like other children. She felt she was the lowest form of human life and was afraid to tell anyone about her Dad. She was sure that her best friend, Ruth, would never speak to her again if the truth were known, so she lied and said that her Dad was working abroad. Eventually, she had to make the terrible confession and was dumbfounded when her friend accepted her as though nothing had changed. She was so grateful that she went with Ruth to church – reluctantly, because she expected to find 'a few old women in woolly hats'. But is was not like that. The people seemed friendly and lively and she heard about the Christian faith for the first time.

Shortly after the separation, Jill's father did go to live abroad, with another woman. Until she was thirteen, Jill believed that her parents would get together again, but these hopes were sorely dashed when her father remarried. On the first occasion when she went with her younger sister to visit him, she had not seen her father for two and a half years. She resented her stepmother; relationships became strained because she would not accept her decisions or recognize her authority. She was disappointed that her father never seemed genuinely interested in her achievements at school. Even when she graduated much later, he did not seem to register any reaction, although she had hoped he would be pleased.

At home, with her mother, things felt better. They became very close, and Jill felt possessive of her. She 'would not tolerate anyone else in my shoes' and had to feel that she was her mother's priority commitment. There were no rows, because she was not 'doing my teenage bit and staying out late at night', but there was no-one to help her to separate healthily from her mother. Finances became strained, and if she wanted new jeans it was 'We can't afford it' or 'Yes, but how are we going to pay for them?' She began to feel guilty now, because she was giving trouble to someone whom she thought she should have been protecting. As Jill grew into her later teens she felt increasingly angry with her Dad. 'It's his job to provide and protect, not mine. I want to get on with my own life. But at least I don't have a stepfather to contend with!' Jill did not miss the father–daughter relationship because she had not had it. Men were significantly absent in her life. She had lived in a predominantly female household.

At university she felt sad and homesick. She joined the Christian Union but had no real sense of God. She said she did not know how to respond to the love of God the Father; she asserted defiantly that she did not need anyone to give her 'a sense of worth' because she felt supported by her mother. All the same, she was quick to interpret any casualness as 'You don't care about me.' 'People don't want me for *me*,' she felt; 'they only want me for what they can get.'

Jill met Terry at university and they eventually married. But her attitude to him was, 'I am not going to expect anything of you or let you expect anything of me. Nice gestures mean that you are trying to buy me. Flowers, and so on, are a trap, making me say things I am not sure about.' It is very hard for Jill to trust herself to another person; she cannot accept that it will not turn out to be a disaster. 'I don't think God wants me to happy. Somewhere along the line I must have done something to displease God. Terry is so important to me that I am sure he will be snatched away' (like Dad).

In the early months of their marriage, Jill is realizing slowly that she has something to give and someone who can cope with her needs. But she sees herself mainly as 'a problem to be coped with' rather than a person to be enjoyed. Jill's next big problem is how to run a family of *two* parents with children. She regards the prospect with much anxiety because she still experiences a family as only having one parent.

Terry also comes from a broken family. He has his difficulties, which are mainly about his total self-sufficiency. His expectations of relationships are low and he puts his trust in high performance. These two young people are far away from their respective homes of origin and most of their friends, but fortunately they are members of a very caring church community. They have joined a home group whose leaders are watchful and sensitive and who will offer help with Terry and Jill's respective and common difficulties in a gentle, unobtrusive manner as time goes by. Home-group leaders have a very important role to play in the lives of young people who are carrying into their own marriage the results of the break-up of their parents' marriages.

Other helpers

Thus far we have been preoccupied with the church, within which we may have some contacts and influence. What about the big world outside? Could we be more responsible about national concerns and policy-making? For instance, there is much public debate about whether or not single mothers should be subsidized to a greater degree in order to enable them to afford appropriate child care. That is all very good, but single-motherhood is only a symptom. We seldom hear the cause being addressed. And until we do, the problem will continue to escalate. In Britain, there are some national Christian organizations which attempt to influence Government policy.[5] In many cities, branches of Christian societies organize local activities to care for the rootless young who wander the streets.[6] Perhaps we would do well to be more interested in and supportive of such enterprises.

17

Healing the hurts

Mercifully, in spite of all the damage done by divorce and other parental disturbance, healing can be found. The Bible is full of repeated assurances that the vital personal presence of God the Holy Spirit will never leave us or forsake us (Heb. 13:5). Whatever our circumstances and experiences, we can be truly certain that we shall never be abandoned or forgotten. That does not mean that we may never pass through difficult periods of doubt, uncertainty or sadness, but it does mean that the God who promises will not break his word.

Healing for children

This loving God who took up our griefs and carried our sorrows (Is. 53:4), and who knows about all our emotional and physical infirmities, is very interested in healing our wounds. As we pour out to him our anger, fear and other feelings about our pain, he will soothe and comfort us. But sometimes it is difficult to get to the point of believing that he is interested and that he will listen and value what we are saying. Why did he let it happen in the first place? There is no known answer to that except that God allows people the use of their 'free' will, and sometimes people want freedom without responsibility. He also allows us to refuse his comfort if we are so minded.

Healing of specific memories is possible and can be helpful. It is important that these memories should cease to be the focus of our awareness, like an unhealed physical wound. Until then this area of our life will always be vulnerable. Healing is about incorporating these experiences into the whole of ourselves. The facts will never change and the scars will remain, but the acute pain of them will be more or less forgotten as healing is complete.

Specific events are usually the outworking of the general atmosphere in which we have been living, however, so there is more than just the actual event to take into consideration when we are thinking about healing. For instance, if parents have divorced, there has usually been an atmosphere of unhappiness first. If there has been some sexual abuse, there has been some sexual disequilibrium between the parents; this must have affected the emotional atmosphere which we have been breathing. As children, we cannot analyse or define our feelings about the atmosphere in which we live. We just experience and live it. Sometimes there are fantasies of distress. It is difficult to distinguish between fact and fantasy when one lives in an atmosphere of pain.

Healing also involves learning to live differently, without the defences which have been erected and preserved so carefully to shield us from unpleasantness. They have to be recognized and dismantled slowly. That can be difficult and can feel very risky. If healing is to take place there must be a willingness for personal change, not just a desire to make the other person change.

There must also be sufficient awareness of suffering to make change desirable. *Healing is not a quick fix.* If we expect instant healing for wounds of this nature, we shall probably be disappointed. Healing is a long, hard journey of growth. Sometimes it seems as though there has been a great healing, and then some of the old reactions will surface again. But if true healing is taking place, these recurrences will probably happen less and less frequently and with less intensity. Miracles of this sort usually happen slowly.

Healing for parents

There are many parents who feel that they have failed their children in spite of all their love and good intentions. Sometimes the parents who are the most conscious of their inadequacies are the ones who least need to feel guilt. But because we live in an imperfect world, there is no such thing as a perfect parent, any more than there is a perfect child. Sometimes we unintentionally pass on to our children the damage that has been done to us.

There are times, of course, when real damage has been done to children, by ignorance, weakness or our own deliberate fault. Healing is still possible, and indeed, relationships can be deepened, when there is admission of failure, repentance and the wisdom and humility to learn from mistakes. Sometimes the damaged relationship has to be patiently repaired, and forgiveness lived out to achieve full healing. Healing is not just getting rid of painful feelings. It is staying with them, bearing the tension and allowing them to speak their penetrating message. We can usually learn more from our sorrows and griefs than from our easy times.

There are some very special passages in Joel 2 in which the Lord refers to the barrenness of the 'years the locusts have eaten' during the troublesome times which the children of Israel had endured. God says, 'Even now . . . return to me with all your heart . . . Rend your heart and not your garments . . . The threshing-floors will be filled with grain; the vats will overflow with wine and oil . . . You will have plenty to eat, until you are full.' This is always God's intention for us if we are willing to admit our failure and ask for forgiveness, but it is not necessarily instantaneous.

Finding oneself

In the process of healing, we find ourselves. There are people who look for comfort and warmth in sex, and who grow increasingly frustrated because they don't get it in a satisfying way, so their search goes on and on. They complain that marriage is wrong when it is really their own failure to find themselves that is at the root of their problem.

Finding oneself does not come from observing morals and standards or conforming to a prescribed code of practice imposed from *outside*, whether it be Christian or any other. It comes from being in touch with our own *inner* centre: it comes from finding our 'heart'.

We may be disconcerted to discover that in our own inner centre there is a hidden well of bitterness, pride, fear, loneliness or total confusion. Then, our 'source of life' produces anxiety, restlessness, endless searching for satisfaction, greed, lust and the other things which make life difficult for us and for the people around us. We must not turn away from this discovery, for we have found something important.[1] We must resist the temptation to cover it up with excuses or greater efforts to be good. This is our heart, whether we like it or not. Jesus knew about our hearts and had a lot to say about them. 'The things that come out of the mouth come from the heart, and these make a man "unclean"' (Mt. 15:18). We can be healed only at the point where we are, not where we are not. If we turn away, we turn away from the possibility of inner healing.

Our heart, as distinct from our brain, is the spiritual organ through which we become aware of our own inner depths – our joys, sorrows, needs and strengths. Through our heart we reach out to God and to other people and become aware of a dimension beyond rational understanding. The whole emphasis of the Christian message is the personal God. When we have found our heart we are in a position to be found by God and to have a personal relationship with him in which we can grow and develop. This has very strong overtones of the foundational relationship with mother, where the 'centre' or 'heart' was established solidly or flimsily. We have to get right back to the very beginnings when we are looking for deep healing and radical change. Since no-one had a perfect start, we are all in need of healing. Some call this 'original sin'.

Healing is about renewing the 'inner centre' so that we are no longer dogged by the things we so dislike. For Christians this is the living, internal *presence* of God's Holy Spirit within our own spirit, loving, forgiving and teaching us. This can make all the difference in our relationships to ourselves and to other people. It can allow us to be real and not go about wearing a mask, trying or pretending to be something we know we are not. It can transform the dynamics of a marriage. When a person has found himself, there will be no need to pursue a possessive search for mothering within the marriage, or for mindless lust masquerading as passion, or for ambitious achievement and many of the other attitudes which upset the balance of a marriage.

Personal fulfilment

The wounds sustained in the impressionable years of childhood may be comforted and healed within the intimate relationship of marriage. This second relationship of intense intimacy has the potential for providing sustenance, growth and personal healing. This is a 'facilitating environment', but, of course, only if it is within a context of reliability and constancy. As Jack Dominian says, 'To make and keep a commitment to another person for better or worse, is not only a means of grace by which they may grow but also reflects something of the character of God's love.'[2] The difficulty is that the child's model and experience of divorced parents have often had a harmful effect on the deep levels of trust, so any new commitment will need very hard work.

The most successful relationships are those in which the two people have found themselves. They then bring into the marriage their own individual wholeness which they can work at in their togetherness. They do not come together to supply fulness for the other's emptiness: they come together to give and to share from their own fulness. Of course, there will be some areas of neediness, but those areas are not predominant features. Divorce usually occurs when people are split inside themselves and are wanting someone out there to meet their own inner needs. Such people are divorced from themselves. The greater the internal split in the individual, the more likelihood there is of a divorce from the partner.

Help in the community

Many can bear witness to the fact that God does heal

our wounds as we tell him about them. But usually healing comes in the experience of God's love through other people as we learn to trust again and to receive and give love. Healing seldom comes in a vacuum.

The primary task of individual churches is to heighten awareness of areas of potential difficulty within their own community and membership, to enable the individuals to be more sensitive to one another, and to create an accepting atmosphere in which people can admit their confusion and need for help without feeling a failure or sensing criticism.

This help could be in very practical terms, such as taking care of the children occasionally so that the parents can have a little more time on their own together. It may be to offer a listening and sympathetic ear (plus the mainly silent tongue) so that the immediate burden can be diffused.

It may sometimes be necessary to help the people to seek some secular professional agency where appropriate help can be obtained. It need not be a Christian agency, but it is essential that the people doing the helping have adequate professional qualifications. Many Christian people fear that their faith may be undermined by such a course of action and that they must stay 'within the fold' for their help, but this is an unnecessary anxiety. No professional person would try to demolish anyone's faith. It may be that preconceived ideas need investigation if they are just a prop or an unconstructive shield against reality, but that would only be done in the context of caring support. Some churches have set up their own counselling centres, and this is a creditable attempt to address the problem, as long as the helpers respect their own limitations.

Many churches have a regular 'prayer healing'

service which is a source of comfort and support to many. The effectiveness of prayer to the God of love, forgiveness and wholeness cannot be overestimated. When the praying is done with someone whose spiritual discernment, concern, restraint and common sense are evident, it can have a very therapeutic effect. Sometimes this is an on-going process which will gently enable deeper layers of distress to be unfolded.

Every family needs external support, from friends, extended family or some section of the community. But in the current climate we are supposed to mind our own business and not interfere with the affairs of other people, even if we can see that they are in difficulties. We tell ourselves that we would not know what to do, and anyway they would probably resent our offers of help because they, too, have absorbed the notion that their difficulties are their own affair. And thus we fail one another in asking and in receiving.

Maureen was thirteen when she became aware of her parents' discord. They still used the same bedroom, but as neither had ever been very demonstrative, the lack of physical affection was nothing new. Maureen knew that over the years her father had been unfaithful. Her mother had always been emotionally fragile and her father seemed to be weak in his own way, pretentious and noisy.

She got up in the morning while her parents were still in bed, cooked her own breakfast, made her sandwiches and saw herself off to school. She was a 'latch-key kid' and arrived home at the end of her day to an empty house. Thus, she learned at an early age to look after herself and become independent. She became a loner inside herself, although on the outside she appeared to be sociable enough. She had little in common with her brother at that stage.

At home, 'sex, warmth and marriage seemed unconnected – three different strands', and Maureen never did see the interrelationship between them. As a result, in her teens she became 'sexually active very early and went off the rails a bit'. She left at eighteen to share a house with a friend and to make her own way in the world. She had been to a good school; she had confidence in herself that she could succeed in life, and she was quite determined to do so. She did indeed succeed, and in due course became a high-flyer. Perhaps the absence of emotional nourishment was to be compensated for by commercial success.

Her father had left the matrimonial home just before Maureen, and the next year the divorce was complete. He formed a liaison with a woman named Gillian, and this caused more difficulties for Maureen. Gillian was very anxious to obliterate all links with her new partner's previous life. Maureen happened to be one link, so she was cut out. They would see each other in the street and he would look away and pass by. Incidents like this were deeply hurtful, and Maureen worried over what she had done wrong to cause such behaviour. She had never been very close to her father, but her relationship with him was closer than that with her mother. In her sadness, hurt and anger, she decided to retaliate. When the time came for her own wedding to a young man she had met at a night-club, her brother gave her away. She did not tell her father until afterwards, when, under pressure from her brother, she sent a cryptic note without surname or address, stating that she was now married.

During her early twenties, Maureen had gone through a time of distress over the break-up of a significant relationship of her own, in addition to the

pains over her parents' divorce. At that time her brother took her to a church that he had been attending. 'Everyone there looked as though they had a secret, and it was a good one,' so she joined an enquirers' group. She eventually joined a house group, and in time this group became her extended family where she was loved and nurtured. It was within relationships there that she gradually became able to peel off one or two of the strong protective coverings and to face some of the deep pain inside.

Maureen and her new husband, Ian, were both Christians by then. They were both products of parents who had been emotionally divorced before actually parting. Both Maureen and Ian were determined that they would not follow in their parents' footsteps. They had problems in the early years of their marriage 'finding moulding points or areas where we could mould around each other, and we fought a lot'. They were committed to the marriage, however, and joined marriage enrichment weekends which enabled them to step back and explore their relationships. They found that they could really trust each other with their hopes and their inner feelings, as well as both wanting to sort out their problems.

Sexual difficulties were an issue for Maureen because of her confusion over sex, warmth and love, and because of her early sexual experiences when she was too immature emotionally. There was also some confusion arising from incidents of sexual arousal with her father. Maureen and Ian received counselling about this, and some areas were loosened up. At a later stage 'the problems were finally resolved through prayer healing'. Maureen began, with tears and pain, to reach towards forgiveness of herself, her mother and her father, and to let go of the past. During all these painful struggles, the vicar's wife (who was a marriage guidance counsellor) stood alongside Maureen and was a 'wonderful support'. Maureen began to be able to integrate sex, warmth and love into her marriage.

Forgiveness for Maureen's father involved the pain of accepting his decision not to see her. She also became able to see him as he really was – a sad, weak man, and not the powerful person he had always seemed to her, as fathers often do. Forgiveness for her mother is coming more slowly, but Maureen's own healing 'has helped me to help her a little to come to terms with her own marriage and its failings.'

Maureen says that these struggles have been a strengthening and enriching experience both for her and Ian individually and for their marriage relationship. 'Marriage continues to be a place of healing for both of us. We have also been useful in marriage preparation courses and marriage enrichment weekends, and in standing alongside other people who have had difficulties.'

In this way Maureen has been able to grow into healing in spite of all her initial pain. As a result she has been able to help various other people to find healing, too.

211

Conclusion

Relationships are the stuff of life. They make our humanity. Subjectively, they stimulate, enliven and nourish us: objectively, they are an endless source of interest and entertainment. If our own or other people's relationships are not sufficiently exciting or convoluted, there are always novels, plays and soap operas; the latter attract a huge watching or listening public. The quality of our relationships affects us vitally. If they are good we are enriched; if they are bad we are impoverished; if they are non-existent we become stunted and deprived in our emotional life. In our relationships we experience – or fail to experience – tenderness, intimacy, conflict, support and struggle. We know and understand ourselves to the extent that we know and understand other people.

Relationships start on the day we are born, and perhaps even on the day we are conceived. From an infant's viewpoint the relationship with his mother initially, and soon with his father, is total, intense, permitting no alternatives and utterly essential to life and survival. From the point of view of an adult, who probably has a busy life going on simultaneously with baby rearing, the relationship may seem tangential. But growing another person and understanding that relationship is the most important task anyone can undertake. This helpless little heap of vulnerability is totally dependent on the ability of the adults whose responsibility he is to nourish him well enough to enable him to grow into a rounded, whole person on every level.

Relationships are not instant. They grow gradually as, little by little, within an atmosphere of acceptance, trust can grow into love, and where all this is confirmed by constantly repeated affirmation. This is, all being well, the baby's first experience of the world of people. As a toddler all this will be cemented through expanding types of experience, to be repeated in a different context during the troublesome stage of adolescence. Eventually, this child will become an adult, capable of deep commitment and responsibility, and in a position to pass on his or her good experiences to the next generation. There will be a good sense of personal emotional solidarity, and the ability to relate to others in marriage or friendship. Here, the true measure of maturity is put to the test! But no-one grows up in a perfect world with perfect parents, so we all have our struggles.

Last week I attended a wedding in Ely Cathedral: two thoughtful people setting out to build a Christian home together. The preacher made a point of saying that in the inevitable tension-points the temptation will be to say, 'I wish my partner would behave differently.' At that point, it takes humility and maturity to be able to say and mean, 'Please help *me* to behave differently.'

We also include the spiritual element in our relationships. Without it a vital element of life is missing and we are only half alive. The basis of the Christian faith is our relationship with Jesus Christ. In his powerful address to the Greek philosophers in Athens, Paul told them, '"In [God] we live and move and have our being." As some of your own poets have said, "We are his offspring"' (Acts 17:28). This is an awe-inspiring thought: we are totally dependent on God, just as the tiny baby's life is wholly dependent on his mother (or substitute carer). There is nothing childish about such dependence. The trouble is that we tend to become so self-sufficient that we cease to be childlike in our relationship with God.

Bianco da Siena knew about the difficulties in relationships when he wrote his beautiful poem in the early fifteenth century. It encapsulates all our relationships, whether they are with children, with other adults, with ourselves or with God:

Come down, O Love divine,
  Seek thou this soul of mine,
And visit it with thine own ardour glowing;
  O Comforter, draw near,
  Within my heart appear,
And kindle it, thy holy flame bestowing.

  O let it freely burn,
  Till earthly passions turn
To dust and ashes in its heat consuming;
  And let thy glorious light
  Shine ever on my sight,
And clothe me round, the while my path illuming.

  Let holy charity
  Mine outward vesture be,
And lowliness become mine inner clothing;
  True lowliness of heart,
  Which takes the humbler part,
And o'er its own shortcomings weeps with loathing.

  And so the yearning strong,
  With which the soul will long,
Shall far outpass the power of human telling;
  For none can guess its grace,
  Till he become the place
Wherein the Holy Spirit makes his dwelling.

Appendix

During my psychotherapeutic training, I had the great privilege of sitting at the feet of the late Dr John Bowlby. He was a psychoanalyst of world renown for his work on the emotional development of children, the nature of the attachment between a mother and baby, and the effects of separation. In his research he built upon the pioneering work of his predecessors and colleagues such as Sigmund Freud, Melanie Klein and others of repute. Now, his work has been built on and elaborated by others in their turn.

The development of a child's personality and his attachment behaviour was something which anyone could observe, but which few people had ever tried to analyse before Dr Bowlby. What goes into the making of the parental bond and why should the disruption of it be so devastating to the young child?

Dr Bowlby's studies, supported by his colleagues, had a profound influence on the institutional care of children in Britain in the 1960s. Previously, children had been admitted to hospital and their mothers were not allowed to visit them, except at short intervals and often infrequently, because it was thought that these meetings were too distressing for the child. The children were left in the care of good and often caring nurses who did all that was necessary for their physical welfare. Naturally, the children cried and were upset when they did see their mothers for the odd hour or two, and were even more upset when their mothers left again. They wanted to go home and be where they belonged, not in a world of strangers.

Where there had been a separation of considerable length, a child would not pay attention when his eager mother returned. Something had happened to the tender psyche, which made the child unable to relate to this 'stranger' who had appeared. It took a while for trust to be re-established, and this proved distressing to both mother and child. On closer observation it became apparent that the damage done by separating a small child from its mother was very considerable.

These researches influenced Government policy, and it is now customary for mothers to be admitted to hospital with their children and to wash, feed and help them in every way possible in order to minimize the trauma of the separation and physical illness. Also, if the mother of a tiny baby needs hospital treatment, the baby is admitted as well, if circumstances allow. This is now standard practice and does not surprise anyone. But it was not always so; much trauma was sustained previously by the mother, but more particularly by the child, in circumstances of separation.

This applies not only to hospitals and other institutions, of course. Any *prolonged* situation of separation creates an emotional earthquake of such proportions for the young child that his attitudes and behaviour in adult life usually bear some marks.

At the same time as Dr Bowlby was working, the late Dr Donald Winnicott was also making some fascinating observations. He was a paediatrician initially, and then became a child psychoanalyst. He had become impressed with the way a child's body and physical reactions indicate his emotional temperature, so he turned to a more detailed study of the child's emotional life. He began at the beginning of observable life and studied the way a mother and new-born baby learn to get to know each other and the subsequent development of that relationship. He coined the now familiar phrases, 'the good-enough mother' and 'the facilitating environment'. As we have seen, a 'good-enough mother' does not mean a perfect mother. Such a person exists only in our fantasy; no mother is perfect in real life. It means a mother who is good *enough* to make life a reasonably comfortable experience and who can provide an environment in which her child can make sense of himself and the world.

I absorbed so much of the teaching of Dr Bowlby and Dr Winnicott that it comes almost as second nature to me; particularly so, because in my clinical practice their observations and ideas have been vindicated time and time again. Of course, fashions and opinions have undergone radical changes since these researches made their first impact thirty or so years ago. Bowlby's and Winnicott's basic principles, however, remain unchanged – probably because in essence they reflect those of the kingdom of God in that their theories were based on the centrality of relationship and love in human growth. It almost seems as though these men and their colleagues were thinking God's thoughts after him. Although Dr Bowlby and Dr Winnicott may, possibly, have been unaware of the fact, I believe that God used them to bring a greater understanding of humanness and the potential relief of much distress. I have quoted much of their work in the book, and, in common with many others, I owe them a great debt of gratitude for all they have done.

I am aware, of course, that in addition to the psychodynamic approach which I follow, other mainstream schools of thought exist (such as the behaviourist approach of B. F. Skinner, H. J. Eysenk and others), as well as dozens of sidestreams. This is not the place for a full-scale examination and comparison of psychological approaches. I have chosen the psychodynamic school because, to me, it seems more effective (as well as more Christian) to address the cause rather than the effect of childhood hurts. However, I know that many people have been helped by other therapies, and for them they may be more appropriate. I do not wish to denigrate them, but simply to state my considered preference.

Notes

1. Families under scrutiny

1. Cited by John Stott in *Issues Facing Christians Today* (Marshall, Morgan and Scott, 1984), pp. 234f.

4. The foundations

1. Joseph Addison, 'When all thy mercies, O my God'.
2. Frank Lake, *Tight Corners in Pastoral Counselling* (Darton Longman and Todd, 1981), p. 102.
3. John Bowlby, *Attachment* (Hogarth Press and Institute of Psychoanalysis, 1969).
4. *Ibid.*, p. 87.
5. D. W. Winnicott, *The Child, the Family and the Outside World* (Penguin, 1964).
6. Mary Loudon, *Unveiled: Nuns Talking* (Chatto and Windus, 1992), p. 130.

5. Separation, positive and negative

1. Alice Huskey, *Stolen Childhood* (IVP USA, 1990); Earl D. Wilson, *A Silence to be Broken* (IVP, 1986); L. Pincus and C. Dare, *Secrets in the Family* (Faber and Faber, 1978).
2. Brian Keenan, *An Evil Cradling* (Vintage, 1993), p. 99.

6. The 'good-enough' mother

1. D. W. Winnicott, *The Child, the Family and the Outside World* (Penguin, 1984), p. 88.
2. M. Esther Harding, *Woman's Mysteries* (Longmans,

219

Green and Co., 1935), pp. 12ff.
3. D. W. Winnicott, *op. cit.*, p. 87.
4. *Ibid.*, p. 88.

7. The absent mother
1. Helen Franks, *Mummy Doesn't Live Here Any More* (Guild Publishing, 1990), p. 5.
2. W. H. Vanstone, *Love's Endeavour, Love's Expense* (Darton Longman and Todd, 1977), pp. 39–50.

8. The father's place
1. Andrew Samuels, *The Father* (Free Association Books, 1985), p. 3.
2. Stephen Verney, *The Dance of Love* (Fount, 1989), p. 74.
3. Eva Seligman, quoted in Andrew Samuels, *The Father*, p. 81.
4. Robin Skynner and John Cleese, *Families and How to Survive Them* (Mandarin, 1983), p. 200.
5. *Ibid.*, p. 178.

9. Fathers, sons and daughters
1. William Appleton, *Fathers and Daughters* (Papermac, 1982), p. 1.

10. When things go wrong
1. K. E. Kiernan, 'Children and Marital Breakdown: Short and Long-term Consequences', *European Population*, vol. 2 (Proceedings of the European Population Conference, Paris, 1991).
2. K. E. Kiernan and P. L. Chase-Lansdale, *The Impact of Family Disruption in Childhood on Transitions Made in Young Adult Life* (Family Policy Study Centre, 1992), p. 18.
3. *The Parent Trap* (Guardian Studies vol. 4), p. 20.

11 Family patterns

1. De'Ath and Slater (eds.), *Parenting Threads: Caring for Children When Couples Part* (Stepfamily Books, 1992). Stephanie Calman contributes one chapter.
2. K. E. Kiernan and P. L. Chase-Lansdale, *The Impact of Family Disruption in Childhood on Transitions Made in Young Adult Life* (Family Policy Study Centre, 1992), p. 18.
3. Peter Harris, *Under the Bright Wings* (Hodder and Stoughton, 1993), p. 152.
4. David Brown and David Atkinson in Christina Baxter (ed.), *Stepping Stones* (Hodder and Stoughton, 1987).
5 Sue Walrond-Skinner, *Family Matters* (SPCK, 1988), p. 131.

12. Ready for marriage?

1. Shakespeare, *As You Like It*, Act II, Scene vii.

13. A marriage that works

1. Kahlil Gibran, *The Prophet* (Heinemann, 1926), p. 16.
2. C. Clulow and J. Mattison, *Marriage Inside Out* (Penguin, 1989), p. 95.
3. *Ibid.*, p. 68.
4. Paul Tournier, *Marriage Difficulties* (SCM, 1967), p. 15.
5. David Runcorn, *Touch Wood* (Darton Longman and Todd, 1992), p. 97.

14. The trauma of divorce

1. Leo Tolstoy, *Anna Karenina* (Penguin, 1954), p. 1.
2. John Peters, *Frank Lake* (Darton Longman and Todd, 1989), p. ix.
3. C. Clulow and J. Mattinson, *Marriage Inside Out* (Penguin, 1989), p. 23.

15. The Bible, children and divorce
1. Italics mine.
2. Joyce Baldwin, *Haggai, Zechariah, Malachi* (Tyndale Old Testament Commentaries, IVP, 1972), p. 241.

16. Preventing the hurts
1. David Atkinson, *To Have and to Hold* (Collins, 1979), pp. 70ff.
2. For example, *Marriage in Mind*, produced by the Church Pastoral Aid Society, Athena Drive, Tachbrook Park, Warwick, CV24 6NG.
3. Sue Walrond-Skinner, *Family Matters* (SPCK, 1988), p. 131.
4. Rosemary Wells, *Helping Children Cope with Divorce* (Sheldon Press, 1993), p. 73.
5. Such as Care Trust, 53 Romney Street, London SW1P 3RF.
6. Such as Frontier Youth Trust, Scripture Union, 130 City Road, London EC1; and Oasis Trust, 22 Tower Bridge Road, London SE1 4TR.

17. Healing the hurts
1. See Myra Chave-Jones, *Listening to Your Feelings* (Lion, 1989).
2. Jack Dominian, *Make or Break* (SPCK, 1984), p. 50.

For further reading

William Appleton, *Fathers and Daughters* (Papermac, 1982).

David Atkinson, *Pastoral Ethics in Practice* (Monarch, 1989).

——, *To Have and to Hold* (Collins, 1979).

John Bowlby, *Attachment* (The Hogarth Press and Institute of Psychoanalysis, 1969).

Myra Chave-Jones, *Listening to Your Feelings* (Lion, 1989).

C. Clulow and J. Mattinson, *Marriage Inside Out: Understanding Problems of Intimacy* (Penguin, 1989).

C. Clulow and C. Vincent, *In the Child's Best Interests?* (Tavistock Publications, 1987).

Andrew Cornes, *Divorce and Remarriage* (Hodder and Stoughton, 1993).

De'Ath and Slater (eds.), *Parenting Threads: Caring for Children When Couples Part* (Stepfamily Publications, 1992).

Jack Dominian, *Make or Break: An Introduction to Marriage Counselling* (SPCK, 1984).

——, *Marriage, Faith and Love* (Darton Longman and Todd, 1981).

Erik Erikson, *Children and Society* (Paladin, 1977).

Helen Franks, *Mummy Doesn't Live Here Any More* (Guild Publishing, 1990).

W. A. Heth and G. Wenham, *Jesus and Divorce* (Hodder and Stoughton, 1984).

Brian Jackson, *Fatherhood* (Allen and Unwin, 1985).

Garry Jenkins, *Co-habiting: A Biblical Perspective*

(Grove Booklets 84, 1992).

K. E. Kiernan, 'Children and Marital Breakdown: Short and Long-term Consequences', *European Population*, vol. 2 (Proceedings of the European Population Conference, Paris, 1991).

Frank Lake, *Tight Corners in Pastoral Counselling* (Darton Longman and Todd, 1981).

Roy McCloughry, *Men and Masculinity* (Hodder and Stoughton, 1992).

Gordon MacDonald, *Magnificent Marriage* (Scripture Press, 1992).

Lily Pincus, *Marriage: Studies in Conflict and Growth* (Institute of Marital Studies, 1960).

John Powell, *Why Am I Afraid to Tell You Who I Am?* (Fount, 1991).

E. Rayner, *Human Development* (Allen and Unwin, 1978).

Andrew Samuels, *The Father* (Free Association Books, 1985).

Robin Skynner, *One Flesh, Separate Persons: Principles of Family and Marital Psychotherapy* (Constable, 1976).

Robin Skynner and John Cleese, *Families and How to Survive Them* (Mandarin, 1984).

Paul Tournier, *Marriage Difficulties* (SCM, 1967).

W. H. Vanstone, *Love's Endeavour, Love's Expense* (Darton Longman and Todd, 1977).

Sue Walrond-Skinner, *Family Matters* (SPCK, 1988).

Rosemary Wells, *Helping Children Cope with Divorce* (Sheldon Press, 1993).

D. W. Winnicott, *The Child, the Family and the Outside World* (Penguin, 1964).

The Church of England Board of Social Responsibility is preparing a report on 'The Future of the Family' which will be published in early 1995.